Leading

without

Heart

Leading without Heart

CORPORATE MALICE HIDING IN PLAIN SIGHT... ONE PHARMACIST'S STORY

DAONDA COMBS-PAYNE

Leading Without Heart:
Corporate Malice Hiding in Plain Sight . . . One Pharmacist's Story

For information about this title contact the publisher:

Pharma Press L.L.C.
www.pharmapress.org
info@pharmapress.org

ISBNs:
979-8-9892062-0-9 (hardcover)
979-8-9892062-1-6 (eBook)

Printed in the United States of America

Document, Document, Document

I never dreamed I would become an author and especially surrounding such an important topic. I am deeply appreciative of the one person in my life that gave me the solid foundation to do so—Dr. Meta Lou Henderson. It was Dr. Henderson who made it clear as a very young and intimidated pharmacy student at Ohio Northern University the importance of documentation. She said, "Document, Document, Document! If you didn't Document it, it did not happen!" How correct she was.

Contents

Introduction

*A*s I sit here pondering what it all means and what went wrong, I am bombarded with articles spotlighting how CVS is launching new programs focusing on access to care. Touting a 24/7 on-demand healthcare portal that would include the ability to schedule mental health services seems inconsistent and disingenuous with the treatment I received as a pharmacy manager with CVS. "Bringing our heart to every moment of your health" as published on LinkedIn by President and Chief Executive Officer of CVS-Karen S. Lynch also seems disingenuous. I stumbled across a Harris Poll commissioned by CVS in March of 2022 that concluded: "42% of working mothers have been diagnosed with anxiety/depression" while "72% don't feel supported at work,"[1] I wonder if that poll included Pharmacists.

Research revealed a refreshing viewpoint concerning women (and was coming from a woman of "Age"). The current CEO, Karen Lynch, shared a story of hope for women during an episode of Fortune's Leadership Next podcast. The interview by Alan Murray and Ellen McGirt was published as follows:

> **Lynch:** Well, I don't know the reason why. But let me tell you what were some of my experiences. When I was young in my career—and this is a great story—when I was young in my career, I walked into a room, and it was all men. And I said, "Where should I sit?" And the guy looked at me and he said, "You should sit over in the corner, because women just take up space in the boardroom."

Lynch: Right. And so that might give you a sense. I share that story because, you know, when I was named CEO, my I came out in a T-shirt and my husband said, You're wearing a T-shirt on your first day as CEO? I said, we're virtual.

My shirt said, "**taking up space**." I shared this story with our diversity council . . .[2]

FOX Business reporter Landon Mion reported on CVS' gender transition guide that now exists. The article[3] published April 15, 2023, revealed that gender transitioning employees **may** have benefits that include medical leave of absence. I hope CVS has changed their policy and will allow FSA funds to cover medical premiums while the employees utilize this benefit, or they "may" find out like I did that they really don't have access to this due to the policy in place at CVS that doesn't allow FSA funds to cover medical premiums while on a LOA seemingly regardless of the circumstances. I could not use my FSA to cover a FORCED LOA initiated BY MY Immediate Supervisor and had to cash out smaller personal IRA accounts to survive.

The transitioning guide, as reported by FOX Business news, states that CVS is "committed to the principle of equal employment opportunity." The guide also stresses that CVS "**won't tolerate** even **subtle forms of discrimination** or harassment in the workplace." This was NEVER enforced upon my immediate pharmacy supervisor in 2016 and what he did was so much more than "subtle," so I doubt it will be enforced now as I will reveal his actions.

My experience as a pharmacist with CVS Health included multiple patient safety issues created by little to no support or support staff. The same is happening today. I do not want to overlook the working conditions, but I am choosing to focus on what should be the most important asset the company has-**the Pharmacist**. The working conditions have been written about extensively, but the health and well- being of the pharmacist has been mostly overlooked and now the conglomerates claim there is a shortage. There is absolutely **NO shortage.** Pharmacists are standing up or changing professions due to the treatment.

I had a promising career at CVS and performed well on the metrics used to justify annual wage adjustments. My performance reviews were consistently above expectations; therefore, I was rewarded monetarily. I would soon realize that the corporate world was driven by profits over working conditions and age was not a virtue nor was being a woman.

I never dreamed I would be a casualty of age and gender discrimination in 2016, nearly 51 years after the **Civil Rights Act of 1964** was enacted, but it happened. CVS claims to be champions for diversity and inclusion, but their actions speak louder than words:

> **"At CVS Health®, we're deeply committed to the work we're doing to develop a diverse workforce and provide an equitable workplace that empowers all colleagues, regardless of their age, ethnicity and background"** as noted on cvshealth. com's home page.[4]

The **Civil Rights Act of 1964** is only as good as those that abide by and defend it. Unfortunately, Lady Justice is no longer blind, and the scales are unfairly weighted with the almighty dollar. CVS seems to have a tremendous reserve built in for reputation defense as a general cost of doing business to prevent the public from learning the TRUTH. My story would be nonexistent and join that of others if I had taken a payout and signed a nondisclosure agreement as Mr. Moretta attempted to persuade me to do.

CVS has self-proclaimed they advocate for mental health but at the same time use unscrupulous practices against their own employees from what I have seen. CVS is reaching towards adding an unlikely place to seek mental health counseling, In-Store, so this is where I will begin, In-Store. Let the (Mental) games begin.

New Age Budgeting

Budgeting for stores in the corporate world does not always make sense. Someone must anchor the ladder while others climb. Pharmacists are not the placeholders of the highly coveted corporate positions but are expected to anchor the ladder. My experiences reveal that Pharmacists are not coveted at all as I became painfully aware of. Mr. Moretta, special counsel of Littler Mendelson for CVS[5], would become a familiar foe although I would come to learn, he had very little to defend because of a working relationship that seemed to have flourished between himself and what was supposed to be my counsel.

I begin this story with the ending of a tough relationship and legal battle that resembled the story of David and Goliath. I refused then, as I refuse now, to let oppression win. I often saw myself being guided by faith, courage, commitment and most of all, heart. My dad always said, "The bigger they are, the harder they fall," I had to fight and have faith. It seems uncanny to me that CVS is using the slogan, "Leading with Heart," when that is the last thing they will reveal as their driving force. Mr. Moretta scoffed at me when I said I want to make a difference for pharmacists, so I hope this sheds some light on some of the behind-the-scenes treatment that gets concealed, similar to how an extortionist prevails by creating fear.

From: DaOnda Payne >
To: John Moretta >
Cc: DaOnda Payne >
November 14, 2022 at 12:58 PM

The beginning

Mr. Moretta,

It has been a very long journey for me and I am glad I was given the opportunity to meet the man/firm behind the many successes of CVS in court. As I said before, I appreciate and Thank you for the bottle of water that was offered to me on your behalf. That spoke volumes about your character. The supposed representation I had was "less than stellar" and frankly should not be practicing.
I have followed the path laid out before me and I now have the truth to the fullest extent that Justice will allow. I do not need to go further for that. Freedom to speak the truth is priceless and that has been afforded to me by a higher up. I have been comforted by the Serenity Prayer and Footprints in the Sand and now I will finish my journey.

Thank you again,

READABLE VOICEMAIL FROM (212) 556-1234

July 30, 2019

> Hello this message is for Ms. Payne Ms. Payne my name is Ellen kibler(?) I'm a reporter with the New York Times and I'm calling you about CVS. I know that you had a lawsuit against a number of years ago and I'm doing some reporting on working conditions in retail pharmacies and was hoping to talk with you. My number is here at work is 212-556-8980 and again my name is Ellen Gable G a BLER and I'm a reporter with the New York Times I would really like to talk with you. Thanks.

REPORTER: Ellen Gabler
MOBILE: (612) 432-0289
WORK: (212) 556-8980
EMAIL: ellen.gabler@nytimes.com

(The previous readable voicemail from our home internet/phone provider was from Ellen Gabler of the New York Times).

Hello? (Call to DaOnda who was currently working at Wright Patterson Air Force Base in Ohio, from Robert- husband in Tennessee)

Hey, you just got a call from a reporter for the NY Times.

Yeah, sure. Next, you are going to tell me Donald Trump called. Serious, a reporter from the NY Times called and left a readable voicemail for you to call her back. She's doing a report on working conditions in the Pharmacy and wants to talk to you.

Really? I'll read it and reach out to her!

January 2012

A new stand-alone CVS was being built at 110 Majestic Grove Rd. in Knoxville, Tennessee that was 5.3 miles from my residence. I was offered the Pharmacy Manager position at this location by John Wilder

(Pharmacy Supervisor). I was currently working at the CVS located at 718 Winfield Dunn Parkway, Sevierville, TN 37876, which was approximately 12 miles from my home and thought this would be a great opportunity and a convenient 5–10-minute drive. I accepted the position.

The new position began with a rocky start. The current Pharmacist-In-Charge Ned Tate was not informed that I was the new Pharmacy manager, and he would have to float to other locations to get his full-time hours. The staff pharmacist, James Dyer, was also unaware of the new pharmacist scheduling requirements to obtain his full-time hours but soon found out that he would have to float as well. The situation was handled in a nonprofessional and unsympathetic manner that led to animosity and a very poor working environment. I did not realize it at the time, but this seemed to be how CVS conducted business to replace older workers and I was soon to be a casualty of this business model.

February 2012

February 2012 came, and the inspection of Store #3743 by the Tennessee State Board of Pharmacy set a precedent for what the Board of Pharmacy wanted to see. The inspection ended with the staff Pharmacist, James Dyer, being assessed a $1,000.00 civil penalty due to the actions of the pharmacy technicians. State Board of Pharmacy rules were broken, and an inspection report was left behind to be addressed by me as the Pharmacy manager, the usual course of business. The report was answered as follows:

DEPARTMENT OF HEALTH
TENNESSEE BOARD OF PHARMACY
COMMUNITY INSPECTION
COMPLIANCE INSPECTION RESPONSE:

INSPECTOR: REBECCA MASON, D.Ph.
(Name changed for privacy)
227 French Landing, Suite 300
Nashville, TN 37243

PHARMACIST IN CHARGE: DaOnda M. Payne, D.Ph. CVS #3743
110 Majestic Grove Rd.
Knoxville, TN 37920
Inspection Date: 2/16/2012
As noted in the Remarks and Recommendations:

"Observed 3 patients picking up prescriptions without being offered counseling. James Dyer (name changed for privacy) was the pharmacist on duty."

Response: CVS has given clear instruction of the role of the technician regarding patient counseling. I have personally spoken with each technician to reinforce the procedures and responsibilities set forth by rule **1140-03-.01** of Standards of Practice. They have been instructed that a **PHARMACIST MUST COUNSEL FACE-TO-FACE EVERY NEW PRESCRIPTION.** After ringing the prescription, the technician is to alert the pharmacist for the need to counsel (currently designated **on all NEW prescriptions** filled at CVS by the words COUNSEL in bold words). At that point they will have met their obligation to be compliant and the obligation then switches to the pharmacist on duty. I have printed a copy of the rule: 1140-03-.01 for everyone to read and sign and to ask questions if need be. I have also printed a copy of the **newsletter sent out by the Tennessee Board of Pharmacy** dated **March 2010** that specifically addressed and answered the questions concerning What Does the Investigator Need to Hear and See! A copy is laminated for future reference and can be found with the inspection form."

Thank You,
DaOnda M. Payne, D.Ph.

James was assessed a $1000.00 civil penalty from the board:

Licensee: James Dyer, D.Ph. Knoxville, Tenn. (Name changed for privacy)
Violation: Failed to provide patient counseling to patients or patient caregivers in accordance with board rules.
Action: Assessed $1000.00 civil penalty

James should never have been in the situation he found himself in. As a pharmacy manager, I was proactive not reactive. Prior to the audit and as a part of the day-to-day proceedings, I laminated and attached the following instructions provided by CVS to the register to assist every cashier/technician in maintaining compliance with the board of pharmacy rules and protect the pharmacist on duty as well as CVS.

For "Mandatory Counseling" POS Prompts:
When a Technician/PSA observes that the Rx label receipt indicates "COUNSEL" and/or one of the prompts for mandatory counseling appear on the register, Technician/PSA must:

- ❖ Inform the customer that the pharmacist will need to speak with him/her.

- ❖ Complete the sale at the register but withhold the prescription(s) that require counseling.

- ❖ Bring the prescription(s) and the customer to the consultation area.

- ❖ Hand the prescription to the pharmacist, not the customer

- ❖ **Inform the pharmacist that a consultation is required.**

For "Offer to Counsel" POS Prompts:
When Technician/PSA sees the prompt for the offer to counsel on the register you must:

❖ Offer counseling to the customer.

❖ Mark "Accept" or "Decline" counseling on the POS screen (if prompted)

Expectations of the Board of pharmacy and CVS in response to the audit concerning the actions of the pharmacy technicians were made **clear** as early as **2012**. Following this visit, a notification was sent to ALL PICs (from the current District manager and Pharmacy Supervisor, Steve Duncan, and John Wilder respectively-names changed for privacy) to inform and warn of the expectations.

Although this was **true in 2012, the narrative would change during 2016 (and be glossed over in 2018)**. Achieving the desired outcome of removing older and higher monetarily rewarded employees while covering up the actions of discrimination and mental abuse by CVS supervisors seemed to have become a priority.

ATTENTION ALL PIC'S:

A NUMBER OF YOU ARE AWARE AT THIS POINT THAT THE NEW BOARD INSPECTOR: REBECCA MASON (name changed for privacy) IS BIG ON COUNSELING!

ON THE FOLLOWING PAGES YOU WILL FIND A COPY OF RULE 1140-03.01 (HER FAVORITE). YOU WILL ALSO FIND A COPY OF THE BOARD OF PHARMACY NEWSLETTER: "COUNSELING; WHAT DOES THE INVESTIGATOR NEED TO HEAR AND SEE."

IT IS THE RESPONSIBILITY OF EACH PIC TO READ, UNDERSTAND AND HAVE EACH TEAM MEMBER READ AND UNDERSTAND WHAT IS REQUIRED. HAVE EVERYONE SIGN AND DATE THE SHEET STATING THEY HAVE READ AND UNDERSTAND AND KEEP IN THE PHARMACY (READILY ACCESSIBLE). GOING FORWARD, ANY TECHNICIAN NOT COMPLYING WILL BE TERMINATED FOR NONCOMPLIANCE.

Rule 1140-03-.01 reads as follows[6]:

RULES OF
THE TENNESSEE BOARD OF PHARMACY CHAPTER 1140-03
STANDARDS OF PRACTICE
1140-03-.03 Medical and Prescription Orders
1140-03-.01 RESPONSIBILITIES FOR PHARMACEUTICAL CARE.

(1) Patient counseling

(a) Upon the receipt of a medical or prescription order and following a review of the patient's record, a pharmacist shall personally counsel the patient or caregiver "face-to-face" if the patient or caregiver is present. If the patient or caregiver is not present, a Pharmacists shall make a reasonable effort to counsel through alternative means.

(b) Alternative forms of patient information may be used to supplement, but not replace, face-to-face patient counseling.

Time at Store 3743 would pass and eventually Ned and James would be completely replaced with Sylvia Oldham (name changed for privacy), a recent pharmacy graduate. "Syl" and DaOnda would become the staff pharmacist and the pharmacy management team at 3743. The store scores improved with the newly paired pharmacists and John Wilder (pharmacy supervisor) retired and was replaced by Rushabh Joshi.

"Rush" was a former pharmacist rumored to have come from Rite-Aid, and he was hired by CVS as the new pharmacy supervisor for district 3602 comprised of 21 stores. Rushabh ("Rush") was sent to store #3743 to train with me prior to assuming the position of Pharmacy Supervisor and to learn the correct procedures for running a store per CVS standards (this explanation was given to me by John- True or Not). Rush was responsible for Year-end performance reviews for pharmacists from that point forward. The 2015 Year-end review (completed by Rush) for Me was as follows and included My overall rankings:

Overall Ranking: District 2/21; Region 8/194; Area 46/1036; Chain 374/7892.

Rumors began to swirl that "Rush" was brought in as a "hitman" to eliminate the older pharmacists who were paid more money. Some pharmacists were even keeping track of how many pharmacists were terminated after Rush arrived. My curiosity was piqued, so I began looking into his background and found that he had graduated from the National College of Pharmacy in Shimoga, Karnataka, India.[7,8] Word in the pharmacy community was that he had come to CVS from Rite-Aid and with no history with any of the Pharmacists in the district, I could see why it would not bother him to destroy lives. Was he really the "Axe" man? Surely, this could not be true.

Tuesday May 3, 2016, As I was working through my shift, I received a call from my son. He informed me that his lab results had come back from his physician, and he was instructed to go to the Emergency Room immediately. The results showed his **Serum Potassium level at 9.3** with the **normal range of 3.5–5.2 mmol/L.** Rush and Jefferson were both at 3743 (where I was currently working) when I received this news. I was forced to have my nephew take my son to the ER since he was there with him, and I was **EXPECTED to remain** on the job **unless I found coverage.** I called my partner, Syl, to see if she could come in and let me leave. Rush was present and was a pharmacist but did not offer to cover me. He simply asked if everything was OK as I left in tears.

Serum Potassium is an important lab value where High potassium (Hyperkalemia) indicates a significant clinical event is occurring involving nerves and muscles including those in the **heart.** Guidelines for a value above 6 require immediate emergency care to determine the cause. Several **fatal** medical emergencies could have been occurring and needed to be ruled out. I stood there in a fog and panic as Rush watched

seemingly emotionally unattached as all the possibilities played out in my head. I could not concentrate and could only think of not being there for my son and not knowing if I would ever see him again alive and at that time every patient in that pharmacy was at risk but neither of those scenarios seemed to bother Rush or Jefferson. It was cruel and unusual treatment—I was trapped and this was **Mental abuse!**

Friday, The Thirteenth CVS Style

*F*riday, May 13, 2016, approximately one week later, a store manager and pharmacy manager meeting was scheduled at the district warehouse at 10008 Parkside Drive, Knoxville, TN 37922. As the meeting was concluding, Rush and Jefferson (Gates-District Store Manager) approached me and informed me that they needed me to stay after everyone else left for an "after the meeting-meeting" even though I was scheduled to return to the store to work the closing shift that night. I had scheduled myself off the morning shift to attend the mandatory manager meeting as EXPECTED by my direct supervisors but looking back, I wonder if my partner was aware of what was about to happen. All pharmacy manager meetings were scheduled without regards to imposing on personal time off and were not reimbursed in any manner. This was the way CVS management conducted business with me-little concern if any for their employee's personal home/work life. I texted Syl to let her know that I would be late for my shift (**did she already know?**):

May 13, 2016, 2:10 PM

In an after the meeting-meeting! Be there as soon as they let me leave.

Ok

The meeting ended and the "after the meeting, meeting" commenced. Once again for the second time in about a week, I was trapped by Rush and Jefferson. It was as if I were being stalked. Rush began by saying that he needed my help at store 6355 on Asheville Highway. He didn't really mean he needed my help and that became evident by his following words that indicated I was going to be **transferred or written up**. I had just recently been given an annual review during which Rush gave me an "Exceeds Expectations," so this was a shock. During my annual review, I was told to go back to the store and when giving Syl her evaluation, let her know that she would be getting promoted from staff pharmacist to pharmacy manager. The promotion would mean **she would be transferred to another location and that I would be getting a new graduate out of** college as my new partner.

Reflecting on the directions given to me by Rush for Syl, I declined **MY surprise transfer** and asked what happened to the transfer that Syl was supposed to be getting and the new grad that I would be getting. I asked why Syl could not be transferred to store 6355 instead of me. Rush responded and said I would get less pushback due to my age. That made absolutely no sense to me, and I had an uneasy feeling, so I asked to be made a floater. A floater travels between stores and is only responsible for what happens at that store during that shift then goes home and is paid for travel. Rush declined the request. I asked why and was told "they" could not do that. I asked again. I asked in another manner- "you cannot do that, or you will not do that? You never have enough pharmacists to cover other stores! You always need floaters!" Rush became visibly angry and said I could remain at store 3743 but, I would be written up and held accountable. I asked, for what? I was not given a response then and I still do not have a response as of today EXCEPT for what John Moretta (CVS Counsel) gave during my deposition in 2018 defending the actions of Rush. Mr. Moretta was making the defense that age discrimination was not the basis for the decision. I was blindsided by the meeting, and I obviously was not prepared to defend myself. I cried all the way back to store 3743 but managed to pull myself together before I got there. I wasn't raised to wear my emotions on my sleeve. I could not believe they got past my armor and were making me cry like a baby. I could not let anyone see what they were doing to me and how it was affecting me. No one would believe me anyway with a recent review of Exceeds Expectations and rankings of:

Overall Ranking: District: 2/21; Region: 8/194; Area: 46/1036; **Chain: 374/7892**

*The manager's comments from Rush on my **2015 Year End***

Performance Review was on repeat in my mind. What was happening? Why me?

CVSHealth:
2015 Year End Performance Review

Manager Comments (Rush)
"**Daonda is a very successful tenured leader** for CVS Health, she **leads** her team **with care and passion, she is always interacting with her pt's** and ensures that her pharmacy **operates efficiently following company** guidelines and **excelling** in most company initiatives. I would want Daonda to approach her team more as a coach and soften her image as a task driven leader. Daonda has been awarded the **best preceptor award** for the district this fiscal. As she mentioned she has had to be very **innovative with her team to deliver consistent results** for the fiscal, she continues to demonstrate behaviors where CVS Health values are an important part of how we accomplish our goals."

In another section of the review, Rush states:
". . . you have leveraged the tools available and fostered the correct behaviors to drive the results in your pharmacy."

". . . As a reflection of your leadership, your store MSH score was 4.1."

YTD myStore Health: 4.1 (Exceeds Target of 3.0)

The Staff Pharmacist is going to be responsible for the Score card throughout the district.

ANNUAL PERFORMANCE RATING:
EE (Exceeds Expectations)

The comments made by Rush in my annual review lay out the fact that **the staff pharmacist and lead technician will now have more responsibilities** going forward; however, that did not seem to be the case when grappling for an excuse to remove me. I was threatened to be **"written up and held accountable" for a store under my leadership that was performing at or above TARGET. There was no LOGIC IN THAT!**

Before the meeting ended, I was told to think about it. What was there to think about? I had a choice of either transferring to a location (store **6355**) with a score of **1.7** or staying at my own location (store **3743**) with a score of **3.1** and being written up. The **target score was 3.0** in the district, and I was exceeding even though I had dropped below **MY NORMAL**. To me, this was a blatant act of age discrimination that CVS would try to defend and disguise. I was being bullied and forced to transfer from a location close to my house that was exceeding district targets to a location that was not meeting targets to get me to quit (**adverse job assignment**).

Multiple calls were made by Rush to my place of employment daily to force me into a decision. I was told I had to decide TODAY at one point. I pushed it off and asked Rush to please stop calling me at work. I informed him it was interfering with my ability to do my job and I would let him know. CVS counsel, Mr. John Moretta, offered the following as explanations (in question form) that I never received from Rush nearly **2 years later:**

```
16          Q    So wouldn't it be reasonable for a
17     pharmacy supervisor to hold the pharmacy manager
18     accountable for decreased performance of a
19     pharmacy?
```

Rephrased:

```
2           Q    So if a pharmacy performance or a
3      pharmacist performance goes down, for a pharmacy
4      supervisor to propose that you can transfer and
5      move to a store that might better fit you right now
6      or stay here and you're going to have to be held
7      accountable, the store is decreasing in
8      performance, that wouldn't be reasonable for him to
9      propose that to you?
```

The U.S. Equal Employment Opportunity Commission website defines Age Discrimination, and it includes JOB ASSIGNMENTS: https://www.eeoc.gov/

Age Discrimination & Work Situations
"The law prohibits discrimination in any aspect of employment, including hiring, firing, pay, **job assignments**, promotions, layoff, training, benefits, and any other term or condition of employment."

The scores relied upon to decide to force a transfer follow. The first one is known as myStore Health. This was a metric that compared performances of individual stores and encompassed several smaller "metrics." The relevant scores for the stores being offered follow in a shortened version of the actual "scorecard." **The story is in the numbers, and they don't add up.**

myStore Health   District 3602

STORE	JANUARY	FEBRUARY	MARCH	APRIL
3743* (My current location)	2.4	1.4	3.1	3.1
6355***	2.8	3.9	3.0	1.7
7246 **	2.5	2.1	2.0	1.9

The overall **District average encompassing 21 stores: 2.6**

The store I was going to be forced to go to and according to Mr. Moretta of Littler Mendelson, **"a better fit" with an Average score of **1.9.**

The location of the store that would be "a better fit" was in Newport, Tennessee (almost **50 miles from my house creating a daily round-trip work commute to increase from 10 miles to approximately 100 miles).

"Move to a store that might better fit you right now."

"you're going to have to be held accountable."

"The store is decreasing in performance."

***Store option given during "after the meeting-meeting" with an overall Average of **1.7.**

***myStore score was STILL ABOVE TARGET and was ONLY below MY NORMAL**

As anyone can see (except my Pharmacy Supervisor and Mr. Moretta of Littler Mendelson), my scores exceeded the scores of the stores that I was going to be transferred to as well as the district average. I will repeat what was a **"REASONABLE"** explanation according to CVS counsel.

"So wouldn't it be reasonable for a pharmacy supervisor to hold the pharmacy manager accountable for decreased performance of a pharmacy."

CVS had policies in place to protect workers and foster better work environments through prevention of Discrimination, Harassment and Retaliation.

B. Anti-Discrimination, Anti-Harassment, & Anti-Retaliation

1. Unlawful Discrimination
"CVS Health is committed to the principle of equal employment opportunity. CVS Health prohibits discrimination against applicants and colleagues on the basis of **race, ethnicity, color, religion, sex/gender**" . . . This policy applies to all terms and conditions of employment . . . **JOB ASSIGNMENTS, DEMOTION, TRANSFER,**" . . . It is our policy to recruit, hire, train, develop and promote the best people available, based **SOLELY** upon JOB- RELATED QUALIFICATIONS.

2. Workplace Harassment
"CVS Health strictly prohibits harassment on the basis of **RACE, ethnicity, color, religion, SEX/GENDER . . . AGE** . . . Engaging in workplace harassment will result in disciplinary action, including immediate termination of employment."
"Harassment of a team member by a **MANAGER/SUPERVISOR,** by another team member, . . . **THREATS** . . . creating an **uncomfortable work environment**, or any other harassing behavior . . ."

". . . if those acts are perpetrated based on colleague's **RACE, . . . SEX/ GENDER . . . AGE . . .**"

The staff I had at 3743 were not all certified and I often had to work outside of pharmacy board rules of 2:1. The following is from the pharmacy board website and explains the ratio allowed between the pharmacist and number of technicians allowed to work at any given time:

"(7) Pharmacy Technician to Pharmacist Ratio (a) The pharmacy technician to pharmacist ratio shall not exceed 2:1; however, the ratio may be increased up to a maximum of 4:1 by the pharmacist in charge **based upon public safety** considerations but **only if** the additional pharmacy **technicians are certified** pharmacy technicians. However, the pharmacist in charge may request a modification of the ratio from the Board in writing which addresses: 1. The pharmacy technician's experience, skill, knowledge and training; and 2. The workload at the practice site; and 3. Detailed information regarding the numbers of pharmacy technicians and the specific duties and responsibilities of each of the pharmacy technicians; and 4. Justification that patient safety and quality of pharmacy services and care can be maintained at the pharmacy. (b) Requested modifications of the established ratios may not be implemented until the written request is considered and approved by the Board.⁹"

I bought study materials through Amazon **with my own money** and worked with each technician to get them certified. I tried to order through CVS, but the ordering budget had been cut off and **I could not get approval from a multi-billion-dollar company**! I didn't have access to the exact Titles, so I had to guess.

$127.51 was too much money for CVS to approve:

November 22, 2015 $59.19   DaOnda Marie Payne

Complete Math Review for the Pharmacy Technician (APhA Pharmacy Technician Training Series)
William A Hopkins
Return window closed on Dec 24, 2015
Buy it again   View your item

Medical Math (Quickstudy: Academic)
BarCharts, Inc.
Return window closed on Dec 28, 2015
Buy it again   View your item

PTCB Exam Study Guide 2015-2016: PTCB Exam Study Book and Practice Test Questions for the Pharmacy Technician Certification Board Examination
Trivium Test Prep
Return window closed on Dec 28, 2015
Buy it again   View your item

PTCB Exam Simplified, 2nd Edition: Pharmacy Technician Certification Exam Study Guide
Heckman PharmD, David A
Return window closed on Dec 28, 2015
Buy it again   View your item

Secrets of the PTCB Exam Study Guide: PTCB Test Review for the Pharmacy Technician Certification Board Examination
PTCB Exam Secrets Test Prep Team
Return window closed on Dec 28, 2015
Buy it again   View your item

The first book I purchased on the list was exactly what was on the list of study materials provided by CVS. I guessed at the rest and bought what I felt would be most beneficial to my current technicians to get them prepped for the technician certification exam.

Monday, May 23, 2016, I texted my decision based on the options given. I chose store 7246 because I knew that most of the technicians there were certified and that would alleviate some of the stresses I had been contending with at 3743.

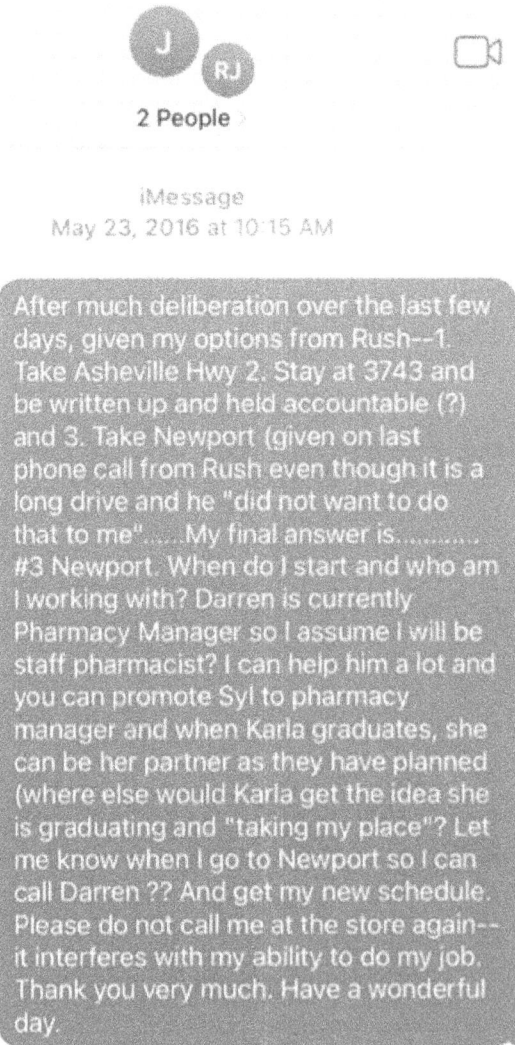

After much deliberation over the last few days, given my options from Rush--1. Take Asheville Hwy 2. Stay at 3743 and be written up and held accountable (?) and 3. Take Newport (given on last phone call from Rush even though it is a long drive and he "did not want to do that to me".....My final answer is.......... #3 Newport. When do I start and who am I working with? Darren is currently Pharmacy Manager so I assume I will be staff pharmacist? I can help him a lot and you can promote Syl to pharmacy manager and when Karla graduates, she can be her partner as they have planned (where else would Karla get the idea she is graduating and "taking my place"? Let me know when I go to Newport so I can call Darren ?? And get my new schedule. Please do not call me at the store again-- it interferes with my ability to do my job. Thank you very much. Have a wonderful day.

Before I had the opportunity to make my decision, I was transferred to store #7246, nearly 50 miles from my house and previous location. Seems as if I did **not** have a CHOICE like Darren did since my transfer appeared on my employee myPersonal Information page on **May 22,2016**- one day **BEFORE** I texted **my response** to Rush and Jefferson. The fix was in, and I was the next target.

JOB HISTORY		
EFFECTIVE DATE	ACTION	JOB CODE
May 22, 2016	Transfer	350124 (Pharmacy M . . .)
May 22, 2016	Data Change (Data C . . .)	350124 (Pharmacy M . . .)

Hey DaOnda. You will actually be the PM at 7246. Darren wants to be a staff pharmacist. We do not want to demote you.

DaOnda

I do not feel it is a demotion. Actually, I feel it is a Promotion. I do not want to interfere with Darren's position since he has been working so hard. I want to help him. You would be demoting him and that is not fair.

He wants to step down and be the staff there. He does not want to be the PM. It's not a demotion because he actually came to us about it.

Since they have not been meeting targets on several metrics--- I would only be removing myself (unwillingly) from a location approximately 5 miles from my home to go to another Location(approximately 45-50 miles from my home) to be in a worse predicament--- look at myStoreHealth--- we have been at 3.1 for 2 months. I dont believe they are meeting target. All of this makes no sense. All metrics cannot be made at all times without a properly TRAINED staff but if I recall correctly, Rush did say that was my responsibility as well- forgive me. I was not told I would be Pharmacy Manager in Newport-- I was only offered it as an afterthought from Rush (at the end of the call). Please honor choice between options given and make me staff pharmacist at Newport effective immediately. Thank you

At this point in the conversation, I believe Rush and Jefferson realized that they were committing Age discrimination, so they tried to rationalize with me. They knew they could not "demote" me, so I had to remain as pharmacy manager at store 7246. What they did at this point was add insult to injury when they forced me to accept the pharmacy manager position at store 7246 but allow Darren to step down AND stay at his location as **HE requested**. Darren was underperforming (1.9) but was granted his request to step down as pharmacy manager AND stay at his home store without penalties. I was forced to transfer (almost 50 miles away) AND assume the liabilities of an underperforming store versus staying at my own store as staff where I was exceeding the target of 3.0 with a score of 3.1.

Remember the evaluation I was given:

"The **Staff Pharmacist** is going to be **responsible for the Score card** throughout the district: TARGET >80." (See Manager Comments 1. Last line). If this were true, why was I being "held accountable" and for scores that were EXCEEDING TARGET?

Darren, a **younger male** Pharmacist, was granted his choice to step down to staff pharmacist with no pushback. In stepping down, Darren was allowed to remain at his store and be relieved of all the additional duties that were expected of the Pharmacy Manager. There was no punishment for underperforming at the level of 1.9 on the myStore Health for Darren but it was "reasonable" for Rush as a pharmacy supervisor to hold me accountable for my store (3743) that had declined yet remained above target of 3.0 according to Mr. John Moretta of Littler Mendelson.

```
4          Q    Okay. Ms. Payne, why did you file
5     this demand for arbitration or this litigation?
6          A    Well, I felt like I was singled out
7     because of my age, due to my multiple complaints
8     and violations, my license.
9          Q    So you filed this lawsuit, you feel,
10    you were singled out because of your age. Okay?
11    Or this arbitration, I should say. Singled out
12    because of your age. What else?
```

"What else?" as if that was not a legitimate reason and was brought without merit.

Page 105

```
 1        A    May -- Friday the 13th of May of
 2    2016. Rush told me that if I didn't transfer to --
 3    he wanted me to transfer to the Asheville Highway
 4    store. I would be written up, held accountable,
 5    and I said, For what? He couldn't tell me for
 6    what. He didn't have any reasoning for that.
 7              I said, Why can't you send Syl to
 8    the Asheville Highway store, because on my review
 9    the whole -- my understanding was that -- and I
10    made notes of that at the time when he was going
11    over the review -- that I was to go back and give
12    Syl her review and to explain that she was, with
13    one other, being considered to be a pharmacy
14    manager and be promoted but that I would be getting
15    a new grad out of school.
16              So I said, Why can't you send her to
17    Asheville Highway? And that's when he said to me
18    that I would get less pushback and that I was
19    older.
```

Truth is, I don't believe Rush had a practical explanation for transferring me therefore, he could not give an answer. Mr. Moretta did his best to defend the inexcusable but failed based on scorecards. This was the ONLY explanation EVER given.

```
 1    employment, correct?
 2         A    I did.
 3         Q    Yes. Okay. So when you chose 7246,
 4    after being given multiple options at 3743 -- of
 5    leaving 3743, one of which included staying there,
 6    correct?
 7         A    Be written up and held accountable.
 8         Q    What would you be held accountable
 9    for?
10         A    I don't know. He never told me.
11         Q    He never told you. Okay.
12              Was the performance of the store
13    going down?
14         A    The performance of the store at that
15    time had gone down some, yes.
16         Q    So wouldn't it be reasonable for a
17    pharmacy supervisor to hold the pharmacy manager
18    accountable for decreased performance of a
19    pharmacy?
20         A    Would it be reasonable to send me to
21    a store that had worse scores? No.
22         Q    Would it be reasonable and actually
23    within guidelines and protocols --
24         A    It's punishing.
25         Q    Excuse me?
```

1   **A**   **That would be punishment.**

2   Q   So if a pharmacy performance or a

3 pharmacist performance goes down, for a pharmacy

4 supervisor to propose that you can transfer and

5 move to a store that might better fit you right now

6 or stay here and you're going to have to be held

7 accountable, the store is decreasing in

8 performance, that wouldn't be reasonable for him to

9 propose that to you?

10   **A**   **It would be reasonable if that were**

11 **done across the board for all of us, but it wasn't.**

12   Q   Why do you believe that was the

13 case?

14   **A**   **I know it was the case because my**

15 **scores were better than Syl's. She was allowed to**

16 **stay there. My scores, I brought the store up in**

17 **7246 from a 1.9 to a 2.8 with a target of 3.**

18   **When I left that store, unwillingly,**

19 **I had a 2.8. Syl had a 2.3. She was not removed.**

20 **She was never told she had to leave. As far as I**

21 **know, she is still there. So I don't understand.**

22   Q   What specifically did Rush tell you

23 about your performance at 3743?

24   **A**   **He didn't, except for my review, and**

25 **he said I was doing a great job. You can read it.**

The transfer seemed to be an obvious move by Rush (the rumored "Hitman") to get me to quit instead of firing me. His actions were **textbook violations of Title Vll of the Civil Rights Act (1964), yet he seemed to be protected**.

I was being assigned to a location that was approximately 50 miles from my home, the scores were not meeting target, a younger male pharmacist wanted to "step down," and it all started at the Friday the 13th meeting with Rush portraying that he needed my help at store #6355 that was underperforming at a 1.7.

I understood early in the process that If I were going to defend myself in any actions taken by Rush, I would have to have a personal file of my performance. I began to keep track of performance-based scorecards to protect myself.

There was a report card titled Colleague Comparison Report. This information was necessary to prove I was being treated differently than my younger partner at store #3743.

The Colleague Comparison Report was a "Tool" used to gage individual employee performance. The reports generally ran behind and reflected employee **performance from the previous month**. Syl received "Full hearts" on Courteous/Professional and Addressed by Name and half of a heart on Satisfied with time to fill (better than my scores) **for June**—all **while on MATERNITY LEAVE**. The reports provided a convenient way to manipulate data. The redacted birth announcement from June follows as proof that Syl was on maternity leave:

is with   •••

June 18, 2015 ·

Happy birthday   Born at 7:53
weighing in at a whopping 6 pounds 15 ounces, 19 1/4
inches. We are so in love!

July 2015

	COURTEOUS / PROFESSIONAL	ADDRESSED BY NAME	ACKNOWLEDGED IMMEDIATELY
Sylvia Oldham	♥ *	♥	♡
DaOnda Payne	♡	♡	♡

This information also included the number of **patients** each pharmacist spoke to and was able to break down barriers to care and **get back on therapy.** The comparison was as follows:

January 2016 Store 3743

COLLEAGUE	# OF PATIENTS	# PATIENTS SPOKEN TO	% STARTED BACK ON THERAPY	ACTUAL # OF PATIENTS STARTED BACK ON THERAPY
Sylvia Oldham	91	11	57.1%	6.28
DaOnda Payne	91	28	48.3%	13.52

January 2016 Store 3743

COLLEAGUE	# OF PATIENTS	# PATIENTS SPOKEN TO	% STARTED BACK ON THERAPY	ACTUAL # OF PATIENTS STARTED BACK ON THERAPY

Sylvia Oldham	126	14	43.8%	6.13
DaOnda Payne	126	47	61.4%	28.86

The ACTUAL number of patients started back on therapy is calculated by multiplying the number of patients spoken to x % started back on therapy.

The percentage alone is **not the focus.** It is the **percentage of** the number of **patients you spoke with** that measures the success of the pharmacist to break through barriers and provide true patient care. The result of the formula is the real metric to be focused on, and **that number is not** calculated and **printed** in the chart- **I added that number that is missing and THAT is** "the rest of the story."

I had more patients back on therapy BUT I WAS FORCED TO TRANSFER?

February 2016 Store 3743

COLLEAGUE	# OF PATIENTS	# PATIENTS SPOKEN TO	% STARTED BACK ON THERAPY	ACTUAL # OF PATIENTS STARTED BACK ON THERAPY
Sylvia Oldham	91	11	57.1%	6.28
DaOnda Payne	91	28	48.3%	13.52

I believe that CVS ultimately created a number system for pharmacists that took the humanity of caring out of the profession. An article in U.S. Pharmacist in May 2020 titled "Pharmacist Burnout and Stress"[10] made a direct correlation between meeting metrics and time constraints with stress and burnout. Pharmacists are human too and deserve to be treated as such- not numbers. Corporate models like this result in negative physical outcomes including cardiovascular diseases, obesity, and mental health as reported in this article. It happened to me, only I lived.

The Tennessee Board of Pharmacy put out a newsletter:

March 2017

News

Tennessee
Board of Pharmacy

Published to promote compliance of pharmacy and drug law

665 Mainstream Drive • Nashville, TN 37243
http://tn.gov/health/topic/pharmacy-board

Board Reiterates That Registrants Shall Have Most Current Edition of the Tennessee Pharmacy Laws 'Paperback Book'

During the January 24, 2017 meeting, the Tennessee Board of Pharmacy stated that the "paper law books are required," referring to the only actual paperback book that is issued by the Board. The current book is the orange-colored 2015 edition. The Board opined on this issue earlier in the meeting, only to reverse the decision before the close of business, as it was brought to the Board's attention that all the information from the actual law book is not published on the Board website. Therefore, a complete electronic copy is not available, and the most current physical book is required. To order, click here for an order form or visit the About section of the Board's website.

Counseling Responsibilities: New Versus Refill Prescriptions

Board Executive Director Reginald "Reggie" Dilliard continues to update pharmacists on the issue of counseling and the fact that pharmacists continue to be disciplined for violating one of the main functions that "shall" be performed by a pharmacist.

Recall that the word "shall" is defined in the Board rules. Per new Board rules signed in February 2017, Rule 1140-01-.01(38) states the following: "'Shall' means that compliance is mandatory."

The counseling regulation, which is located in Rule 1140-03-.01, indicates that a pharmacist shall counsel on all new prescriptions. It is not acceptable to simply ask if a patient has any questions on a new prescription. Refer to Section 1140-03-.01(1)(e) for the eight points of counseling and remember to use professional judgment as stated, in part: "Patient counseling shall cover matters, which in the exercise of the pharmacist's professional judgement, the pharmacist deems significant . . ."

A new medical or new prescription order may include, but is not limited to, the following:

♦ A prescription medication that has never been taken or used before by a patient.

♦ A prescription that has been reassigned a new prescription serial number as refills are no longer available from the original prescription due to expiration, refill quantity used to completion, or discontinuance by the prescribing practitioner, among other legitimate reasons.

♦ A prescription that is in, as an example, Schedule II, such as amphetamine salts, and therefore is always a new prescription.

♦ A prescription that is written for a prescription device such as an auto-injector or oxygen concentrator dispensed from the pharmacy.

Be advised that a new prescription shall always be counseled face-to-face by the pharmacist unless the patient or caregiver refuses counseling to the pharmacist. Furthermore, the pharmacist may still be held in violation if the patient or caregiver refuses, but does not do so face-to-face to the pharmacist. A refusal to counsel to the pharmacy technician does not meet the requirement on a new prescription.

Moving on to the refill as stated in Rule 1140-03-.01(1)(f), "Upon the receipt of a request for a refill of a medical or prescription order, a pharmacist or a person designated by the pharmacist shall offer for the pharmacist to personally counsel the patient or caregiver." Therefore, counseling as described in (e) may not be required unless deemed necessary by the pharmacist. However, the offer for the pharmacist to counsel is still required.

Pharmacist-in-Charge Position Adds Large Responsibility

So, you are fresh out of pharmacy school, or maybe you are an established pharmacist and feel the call to move to a position that at times brings additional compensation or benefit, or maybe the current pharmacist-in-charge (PIC) has unexpectedly been disabled or terminated or has moved for a better opportunity. Regardless of the case, it is strongly

TN Vol. 19, No. 1

Page 1

continued from page 1

advised to review past Board minutes, live streaming videos of Board meetings, and Board regulations so that you may better understand the PIC responsibilities. The PIC may be found accountable, and many times disciplined by the Board, for actions including negligence of theft or loss of drugs (not auditing controlled substances (CS) consistently), failure of self or of other employees to counsel patients or offer for the pharmacist to counsel patients, lack of a sink with hot running water, lack of a functional refrigerator, lack of or not following standard operating procedures, not following sterile compounding rules and regulations, lack of proper staff training, cleaning, and other required documentation, lack of drug removal due to adulterated/expired drugs found on shelves, and the finding of pharmacy technicians with expired registrations, among other things. Discipline may include, but is not limited to, a letter of instruction, letter of warning, reprimand, probation, suspension, or revocation. These violations become a permanent record in your pharmacist license file. Except for the letter of instruction or warning, other violations will be made available for public view. Costly civil penalties may also be levied by the Board. **Even if you did not directly commit the violation** (eg. failure to counsel or technician registration expired), violations may result against the PIC's license.

In this newsletter, the board strongly advises anyone accepting the PIC position to fully investigate the responsibilities of that position **BEFORE accepting. I was not given that choice** nor was I granted my request to become a floater. Was I FORCED into the position for NEFARIOUS reasons?

The following is some information I found and is taken directly from a reporter for Insider by the name of Rebecca Knight, November 24, 2022

"A 2022 survey from AARP of nearly 3,000 of its members found that roughly two-thirds of workers over the age of 50 said they believed older employees face age discrimination at work;

What's more, older workers who were unemployed for six months or more had far worse outcomes in reemployment, including 59% who made less money than in their previous job.

To prove age discrimination, you have to show that your age was the difference between being hired and not, as opposed to some other legitimate rationale.

Last year, the EEOC resolved roughly 13,000 age-discrimination charges filed against employers. Of those cases, only **18%** were found in favor of the employee."

". the employer would have to then explain why they made the decision they did."[11]

Keeping Score

I began my newly assigned position as Pharmacist-In-Charge (PIC) at store 7246. I was relieved to know that I was approximately 50 miles from the CVS warehouse in Knoxville where the district offices were located and the home to Rush's office. I felt the likeliness of frequent visits from Rush and the harassment would stop- out of sight, out of mind. I was still in the mindset of defense so I continued to keep track of report cards (Metrics) that I thought would protect me.

I decided I needed a baseline, and the best report would be the Colleague Comparison Report again. I started store 7246 at the end of May 2016 so I knew I would have to wait until July 2016 to get any numbers. The first report with all 3 pharmacists on it during the transition period was July 2016. In this report, the numbers reflected the same work ethic for me and results that I had at store 3743. My performance was equal to or greater than either of the younger male pharmacists. I talked to more "eligible NSP patients" and got more patients back on therapy than either of the younger men. I was making a difference in patients' lives. **I was "leading with heart."**

Every day that I went to work, the words Rush said were tolling on me mentally. I kept wondering why he said I would be written up and held accountable. I started keeping track of more scorecards. This time I would change my strategy-I would keep track of store comparison performance metrics so I could gage my overall store performance at

7246 vs. 3743 where I was just forced out of and replaced with Syl (my younger pharmacist partner). I had to make a case for myself, I had done nothing wrong. The transfer to the Newport store revealed the same performance for me.

Store 7246   June 2016

COLLEAGUE	# PATIENTS	# PATIENTS SPOKEN TO	% STARTED BACK ON THERAPY	ACTUAL # OF PATIENTS STARTED ON THERAPY
Darren	65	12	76.5%	9.18
DaOnda Payne	65	18	65.2%	11.74

Store 7246   July 2016

COLLEAGUE	# PATIENTS	# PATIENTS SPOKEN TO	% STARTED BACK ON THERAPY	ACTUAL # OF PATIENTS STARTED ON THERAPY
Darren	69	10	83.3%	8.33
DaOnda Payne	69	27	54.8%	14.79

One of the first metrics I focused on in my "new" location to compare and justify my removal from 3743 was a personalized report that aided the pharmacist and focused on increasing care for patients with multiple chronic health conditions or complicated medication regimens.

As I recall, the first report 6/09/2016 revealed Store 3743 (where I was forced out of) 0% calls were completed and Store 7246 (my new location) had 100% calls completed. I was outperforming my previous location (where I was going to be written up and held accountable for performance issues-as suggested by Mr. John Moretta) but (remember!), "The **Staff Pharmacist** is going to be **responsible for the Score card** throughout the district: **TARGET >80**." (See Manager Comments 1. Last line). If this were true, why was I being "held accountable" and for scores that were **EXCEEDING TARGET?**

The report from 11/12/2016 revealed Store 3743 (my ex-store) at 0% again (No attempts were made to make the calls) but Store 7246 (my current store) was at 100% (all calls made). No changes in PIC at my previous store (3743) were made by Rush at this time due to per-formance issues- odd.

The next scorecard I managed to compile information from was called **myCustomer Experience**. This scorecard included a multitude of smaller metrics. I put together a chart to show the progression of the scores between 3743 (where I was forced to transfer out of) and store 7246, where I transferred to **DUE TO MY PERFORMANCE**.

STORE # 3743		STORE # 7246	
Pharmacy Manager		Pharmacy Manager	
Sylvia Oldham		DaOnda Payne	

DATE	SCORE	TARGET	VARIANCE	DATE	SCORE	TARGET	VARIANCE
6/22/16	69	85	-16	6/22/16	77	89	-12
8/1/16	73	85	-12	8/1/16	98	89	9
8/8/16	76	85	-9	8/8/16	92	89	3
8/19/16	76	85	-9	8/19/16	88	89	-1
8/29/16	76	85	-9	8/29/16	91	89	2
10/11/16 8:08 pm	76	85	-9	10/11/16 8:08 pm	86	89	-3
10/11/16 8:09 pm	73	85	-12	10/11/16 8:09 pm	94	89	5
11/14/16	78	85	-7	11/14/16	92	89	3

June 26, 2016, was the first available score after my forced transfer in May 2016.

The first score above (6/22/16) for 7246 was still reflecting the negative numbers from the past performance under the previous PIC who was granted his wish to step down. I was facing a higher TARGET than 3743 but managed to eventually bring it to a positive; unlike 3743. Looks like Rush was onto something with the performance issues, **but the numbers do not lie, and the issues were not mine.**

myStore Health metrics trended in the same direction. myStore Health in March and April 2016 (right before I was forced out) were 3.1 with a target of 3.0. March and April at Store 7246 sat at 1.9 and 2.3 with a target of 3.0, but **I was going to be written up and held accountable for performance**-sounds believable.

By September, 3743 (where I was forced out of) had an Rx rating of 2.5 and 7246 (my new location) had an Rx rating of 2.7. October showed an increase at 7246 (my new location) to 2.8 and a steady but still not at target score of 2.5 at 3743 (where I was forced out). **Overall, 3743 went from 3.1 down to 2.5 (after I was forced to transfer due to performance) and 7246 (my new location) went from 1.9 up to 2.8.** I was once again outperforming my old store and younger ex-partner.

My patient care scorecard would not disappoint. In November 2016, **7246 (my new location) took number one in the district** with an **impressive 93! Rush tweeted** this out but **NEVER congratulated ME** once. The award was presented to my lead technician-not me. I had no support from my supervisor, but he did manage to make me feel less than professional and largely overlooked. I am sure the feeling was similar to Ms. Lynch in the boardroom—"**taking up space.**"

There definitely was no positive feedback. I still to this day look at the quotes Rush posts on his Twitter page with the most current being:

"If you're complaining you're not leading. Leaders don't complain. They share a vision. They inspire with optimism. They focus on solutions" but **I only hear him say to me, "You would be surprised what you can say/do when you take emotion out of it."**

Rushabh (Rush) Joshi @rushjo... 12/11/16
Team 7246 impacting patient lives ...My Patient Care @93 for Nov.

I tried to keep my sights focused on what I was there to do and who I was there for, the patients. I was devastated after being forced out of a store I put my heart and soul into. The forced transfer was definitely taking a mental toll on me. I found comfort in the people I served, the patients. I kept several of the compliments I received directly after being forced to store 7246. Some examples follow:

 ***Only Jefferson and David responded, not Rush** (my pharmacy supervisor)

Dave wrote in a letter:

June 6, 2016

Daonda Payne Pharmacy Manager CVS #7246
346 Cosby Rd.
Newport, TN 37821

Dear Daonda,
I recently received a customer compliment regarding your store and wanted to take a minute to say, "Thank You" and job well done! I really appreciate the positive impact you are having on Customer Service in your store.

Below is an excerpt from that letter:

"RPh Daonda is amazing, she truly cares about her patients and is absolutely outstanding."
Thank you very much for making customer service a top priority. I am proud to have received the compliments and appreciate your efforts in demonstrating **Caring, Empathy** and **Trust** with your patients!
Again, congratulations and keep up the great service!

Thank you, David Sanford
Regional Manager

cc: **Jeff Gates** w/Attachment (5949658)

*Notice that Rush was not cc'd (very ODD AGAIN)

Dave wrote in a letter:

July 18, 2016
Daonda Payne Pharmacy Manager CVS # 7246
346 Cosby Hwy.,
Newport, TN 37821

Dear Dayonda,
I recently received a customer compliment regarding your store and wanted to take a minute to say, "Thank You" and job well done!

Below is an excerpt from that letter:

"Customer says they went to store and needed their medication: had filled it recently and could not find it. Customer talked to RPh., who would call the insurance company to see if she could do an override. It took time to do this, but she was so kind and patient to get this taken care of. She needs a pat on the back for going above and beyond."

Thank you very much for making customer service a top priority. I am proud to have received the compliments and appreciate your efforts in demonstrating **Caring, Empathy,** and **Trust** with your patients!

Again, congratulations and keep up the great service! Thank you,

David Sanford Regional Manager

AGAIN Jefferson was the ONLY one Dave Cc'd-NOT Rush (the PHARMACY SUPERVISOR) AND if sending praise to an employee, the management should at least spell the name correctly

I♥Customer   **my♥Impact**

Congratulations, You've GOT Heart!
Daonda Payne

Congratulations on providing your customers with legendary myCustomer service!
By providing excellent customer service, you are impacting your customers' lives and helping them on their path to better health.

You have the opportunity to make an impact on your customers' lives and their feedback reflects the outstanding service that they have received from you in your store. Celebrate your achievement and the impact that you have in your store.

October, 2016

Manager's Signature

Pharmacy

♡♡♡♡♡♥♡♡♡♥♡♡
JAN FEB MAR APR MAY JUN JUL AUG SEP OCT NOV DEC

Use this QR code to visit the
Values in Action website

DaOnda,
Thank you so much for being an awesome
preceptor and not making this rotation any
harder than it needed to be, I really
appreciate you taking time to teach me
the important things that I needed to
know. I really feel like you made this
rotation about me and did not just use me
as free labor :) I do not believe I
would have had the same experience at
another pharmacy, and I don't think I
would have learned as much.
            Thanks again!! ~Morgan

*Sentiments on a card from one of my pharmacy students during rotation.

REGION 36
focus

Store 6361 Sevierville, TN

"I wanted to make a comment about Daonda Payne. She works here in TN. I wanted to tell you what a sweet person she is. I had no money and the prescription I was given was $600. She called the drug company that makes them, and they are going to help me. She is a super lady! I was just calling to do a price check and she offered to help me. She did this all after work on her own time! '

Thank

Thank

Thank

Darida,
I cannot Thank You Enough
For helping me, one stressed
out Lady who   Forgot
My Suitcase, with   My
Scripts. It's meant we could
contd. Our Trip & Not be worried
or feel bad. You didn't
have   ) To give me these
or   Even help but you
were/are So Kind & I'll always
Remember your Random act
of Kindness.
My best To
You,
Kathy Williams
NC

You

You

You!

Darren
A Beacon of Hope

*D*arren was the pharmacy manager at store 7246 that was asking to step down from pharmacy manager to staff pharmacist. I did not want to be pharmacy manager because I knew all the responsibilities that came with it, and I knew that it would be easy for Rush to find something to pin on me since this store was underperforming and he had already threatened to "write me up and hold me accountable" at store 3743 even though we were exceeding target. I was surely facing circumstances that were going to be hard to overcome.

Darren and I got along well, and Darren was at the warehouse on Friday, May 13, 2016, when Rush and Jefferson ambushed me. He had stayed over to talk with them about something, but I did not ask what. I never thought at that time we were going to end up partners at a store. Darren was kind and consoled me before I left the warehouse to go back to work for the closing shift at 3743. He told me he would stand by me if I needed him. I would soon need him.

Darren was supportive when I began working at store 7246 with him. He knew how I was being treated by Rush. He told me he had seen an article in Drug Topics about lawsuits being brought against CVS concerning metrics and it sounded like what was happening to me. He gave me the name of the attorney, so I looked it up.

I found the article and the attorney representing the pharmacists in the lawsuit.

The attorney was Jarrel L. Wigger of the Wigger Law Firm, Inc. located in South Carolina. After reading the article, I determined Darren was right. It sounded a lot like my situation, so I called Mr. Wigger. Everyone at store 7246 was supportive and knew Rush had treated me unfairly. They were aware of my scores and their own. We became a great team, and our scores began to improve and surpassed my previous store 3743. As we improved, store 3743 declined.

The team encouraged me to file against CVS. Darren and I rearranged the pharmacy schedule that allowed me to make an appointment with Mr. Wigger on July 5, 2016. My sister, a CVS technician at another store, went with me. We drove to South Carolina in July, met with Mr. Wigger, and drove back with few people knowing. I was blessed to have a supportive team and relieved to hear Mr. Wigger answer my question: What are the odds that CVS will be held accountable for their discriminatory actions, and something be done? He replied with a short answer: "I win." I was instructed to not take any more meetings with CVS alone. I was to call him FIRST.

Article: March 27, 2015

The article printed by Drug Topics March 27, 2015[12] would be an article of interest. The article detailed a lawsuit against CVS by 4 former CVS pharmacists. I did not know it at the time, but I was about to get real familiar with this case and the litigants.

In the article, the pharmacists were alleging that **CVS was using their metrics** system to **terminate older pharmacists who were higher paid**. The pharmacists point out that it is near to impossible to meet both CVS metrics and comply with the law. The metrics system is cumbersome and saddled with time constraints. Each required activity laid out by the boards of pharmacy such as counseling ALL NEW prescriptions among many other tasks increases the likelihood of not meeting the metrics or not meeting the requirements of the law.

Michael DeAngelis, who is a spokesperson for CVS, is quoted in the article and maintains that any of the allegations made by the pharmacists have no merit. He makes claims that the **metric system** in place by CVS is only **a tool** provided to the pharmacist to **HELP** them. According to Mr. DeAngelis, the metrics system adds effectiveness. Services to the patients and expectations of the patients are driving factors in the development of the system.

The four pharmacists all had a similar story of being discriminated against and losing their job based on the metrics system that was supposed to be an aid in managing tasks and being more efficient and effective in taking care of patients.

It is my belief that Rush did not properly grasp the concept, or the **purpose of the metrics** as **stated by Michael DeAngelis:**

"Like other companies, we measure the quality and effectiveness of the services we provide to ensure we are meeting our customers' expectations and helping them achieve the best possible health outcomes."

"**Our systems are designed to help our pharmacists** manage and prioritize their work to best serve their patients."

The metrics were not intended to be a tool for punishment or replacement, they were intended to "**help**" the pharmacist. My case was not about metrics, and it seemed to be getting lost even by what would be my new counsel. **My case was about AGE DISCRIMINATION and PROVEN BY METRICS.**

Michael DeAngelis was on the right track. The metrics were to HELP the pharmacist. and indeed, they helped me prove the discrimination occurring by comparing my performance to the younger pharmacists at both locations, store 3743 and store 7246. The narrative of performance issues was just not standing the litmus test, So, a new crisis would soon emerge and continue to shift the blame to me.

While all the fuss was going on about my performance and scheduling, I was faced with other challenges involving inventory. The counts were over and under and had to be corrected. I spent much of my time communicating concerns with LP (Loss Prevention) and initiating counts that triggered investigations. I must have been the only pharmacist following the procedures of counting and back counting all controlled substances.

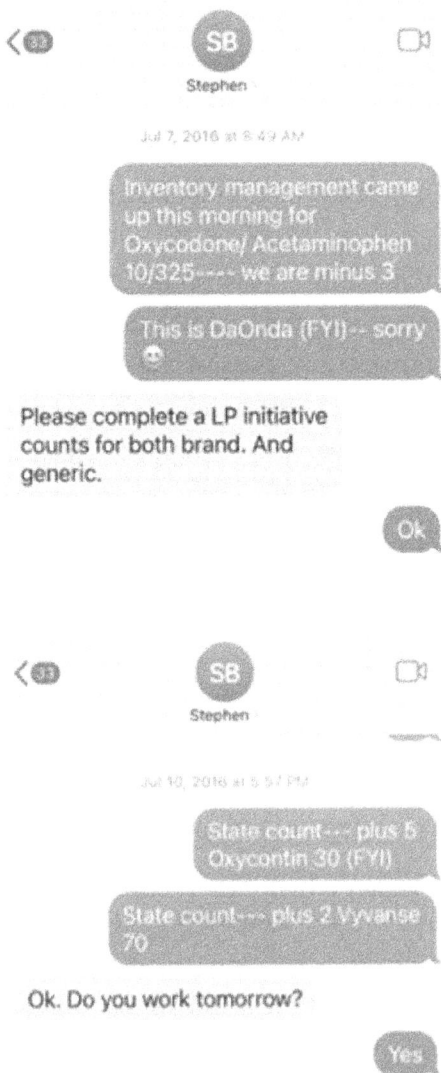

SB
Stephen

Jul 11, 2016 at 4:23 PM

Filling a prescription for Oxycodone 5mg----- plus 10 BOH (FYI)

SB
Stephen

Aug 7, 2016 at 9:59 AM

When doing state counts, +10 on Oxymorphone ER 20. How do you want me to proceed to reconcile?

Aug 7, 2016 at 11:25 AM

Yes. You can also complete a LP Initiated counts.

Ok

Aug 11, 2016 at 8:12 AM

Mandatory Inventory count In Hydrocodone/Apap 5/325--- over by 16. How do you want me to handle it??

Please complete a LP initiated count on both brand and generic on Norco 5/325. All NDC's. What store number?

SB

Stephen

Sep 5, 2018 at 2:12 PM

CompleTe a LP initiated counts at closing. Need to report it on initial notification. I'm

Sep 5, 2018 at 4:17 PM

I already reconciled under pharmacist count error-- how can I change it ?? Is it possible?

Correcting the inventory in Rx connect has to be done. Don't change it you still have to report the shortage by completing an initial notification.

I corrected the count but used pharmacist count error.

Ok.

SB

Stephen

Oct 20, 2018 at 10:00 AM

Filling a prescription for Focalin XR 20----minus 30 but Focalin XR 15 shows BOH of 30 when we have none. Trying to back track now by calling the patient and have them look at what they have but no number in computer. Looking for hard copy, so I am going to correct the count on Focalin XR 20 under pharmacist count error. How would you like me to proceed after that??? Focalin XR 15 is still off. Should I make it zero like it should be?????

Please do LP initiated counts for the two strengths both Generic and Brand.

Please let Rush know.

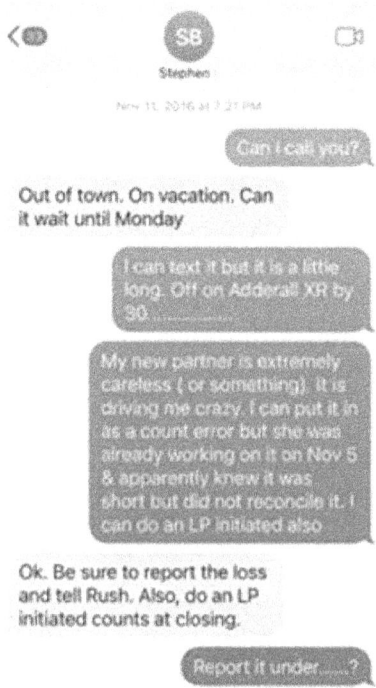

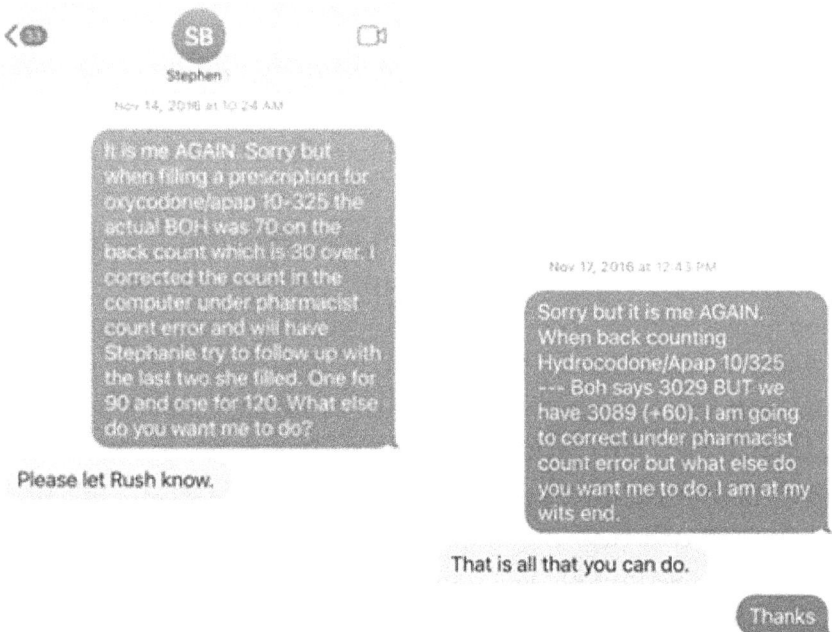

> Rush,
> On 9/2/2016 Charlotte filled a
> prescription for Morphine Sulfate ER 30
> for a patient. It was for #90 and
> everything was correct but she shorted
> the patient #30. I found it on a state
> count 9/4 and touched base with Steve
> on how to handle it. He said to try to
> figure out who was shorted and go from
> there but I Had To correct the count at
> that time. Well, I called the patient who I
> thought it belonged to and left a brief
> message. She never called back because
> she didnt listen to her messages. She
> finally called to say she thought she was
> shorted and I verified that today. I let
> Steve know the results and he said to
> correct the count again and do a misfill
> report for shorting the patient. I am
> working on that now so if I need to do
> anything else or something different let
> me know. Steve said to let you know

From June 30, 2016-November 17,2016 the previous text messages occurred. They are only a few of the times I had to contact Loss Prevention concerning overages and shortages of narcotics. All of this led to more reports that were mandatory for the DISCOVERING PHARMACIST to complete.

My current partner, Darren and my new partner, Steph Elm, appeared to not be following procedures. They did not relay information to me willingly; I had to find it myself. I reported my concerns to LP- that's all I could do. Rush seemed to never be available and if he was, he was nonresponsive. **His only concerns appeared to be rooted in MY PERFORMANCE.** All of the **extra reporting THAT THE DISCREPANCIES** WERE creating was **causing me to struggle with** all other **metrics** such as: satisfied with time to fill, ready when promised, waiters verified before promised time, etc. I triaged and decided being compliant with narcotic reporting and DEA guidelines was most important. I did not think it would be a good look on my license to have unexplained and undocumented narcotic discrepancies- both overages and shortages. I was also concerned with the hearsay from the technicians that some of them were less than honest and I would find out much later my concerns were warranted-an arrest of one of the technicians for stealing Xanax would follow.

A New (Manufactured) Crisis

*D*uring my first few weeks at 7246, Darren continued to make the pharmacist schedule which accommodated his obligations to the board of pharmacy. Soon, I became responsible for making and posting the schedules for pharmacists and technicians. I was informed by our district scheduler, we had to have 3 split days a week and were not allowed to have 2 back-to-back long days. This was a surprise to me since **THIS store** (Darren and Stan) had been working a very different schedule than the mandatory schedule that was supposed to begin November 1, 2015, and it was now August 2016. This seemed like a direct initiative by Rush to place more burden on me and make me drive over 100 miles/day-EVERY DAY OF THE WEEK to be compliant with the scheduling or he would have an excuse to fire me.

In October 2015, all Pharmacists were informed we were expected to be 100% compliant with scheduling requirements. The requirements included splitting shifts 3 days a week and we were not allowed to work 2 back-to-back long shifts. While still Pharmacy Manager at store #3743, I received notification from our district scheduler concerning these scheduling requirements. Syl and I had a conversation about the scheduling:

Oct 28, 2015, 12:32 PM

Marge Ellen called— we have to split 3 days a week.

Great. Certain days or whatever we come up with? And starting when?

Starting Nov. 1 that is all I know

I just called her & she said as long as we're splitting 3 days it doesn't matter which ones. So we can probably still work Friday-Saturday weekend.

I penned an e-mail to David Sanford (supervisor of Rush and Jefferson) to clarify scheduling and to verify whether there could have been or could be an exception to the mandatory scheduling requirements for store 7246. The e-mail follows:

Pharmacist Schedule - Payne, Daonda   https://storemail.cvscaremark.com/owa/#viewmodel=Re...

Pharmacist Schedule

Payne, Daonda

Wed 8/17/2016 11:40 AM

To Sanford, David W. <David.Sanford@CVSHealth.com>

Good morning!

I hope I am not intruding but I have an important question and I trust you can lead me in the correct direction. I have recently changed locations and now I am having to drive approximately 1 hour to work and 1 hour home every shift verses the previous 15 minutes (in heavy traffic! lol).

I have been given directions through Marge Ellen from Rush that we have to split our shifts. I am wondering, under the circumstances, if it is acceptable to alternate days (eliminating the 2 back to back long days) in order to offset the travel time. My partner drives 1 hour as well and this would be a great relief. If no, what are the corporate requirements for scheduling since it seems to be different at most locations. Any help would be greatly appreciated so I can be compliant.

Thank you for your time,

DaOnda Payne, DPh
Store #7246 (Previously #3743)

David Sanford @dwsanfordcvs · 7h
You are what you do, not what you say you'll do.

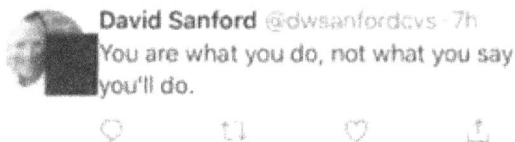

Copies of the Pharmacist signature pages for each shift the men had been working revealed the mandatory scheduling guidelines were not being followed. The emphasis and URGENCY Marge Ellen put on the COMPLIANCE WITH THE MANDATORY guidelines from Rush suggested there may be an exception to store 7246 due to the travel distance and the fact that noncompliance had been occurring since at least December 27, 2015. Dave never responded to my e-mail but delegated the task to Jefferson. Jefferson made the call to me to inform me that there were absolutely NO EXCEPTIONS and if the schedule was entered in the system as compliant but worked another way, immediate termination would occur. I had only been at store 7246 beginning around the end of May 2016 and Darren, and I were working the same kind of schedule he and Stan had been working but, there was one difference- I was the other pharmacist now not Stan. This scenario presented Rush with a new angle and something solid he could sink his teeth into-**scheduling noncompliance that would lead to my immediate termination.**

Inspection of the pages of the daily pharmacist signature logs that every pharmacy is required to keep showed NO split shifts beginning

12/27/2015. The signature logs are a requirement by the state board of pharmacy and are outlined in 1140-03-03 as follows:

STANDARDS OF PRACTICE CHAPTER 1140-03 (Rule 1140-03-.03, continued)

b) Each individual pharmacist using a computerized system in the refilling of a medical or prescription order shall certify that the information entered into the computer for such a refill is correct by verifying, dating, and signing a hard-copy printout of each day's medical or prescription order refill data, or in lieu of such a printout, by signing a statement in a book or file each day attesting that the refill information entered that day has been reviewed by the pharmacist and is correct as shown. Such documentation shall be separately maintained at the pharmacy practice site for at least two (2) years from the date of the last dispensing.

The store hours of operation were:
M-F: 8am-9pm; Saturday 9am-6pm and Sunday 10am-6pm.

The pharmacist signature log was a simple thin booklet, and the pages were bound and a statement that was compliant with the board of pharmacy was at the top of each page and stated the undersigned pharmacist attested that all prescriptions and prescription data entered on a specific date were reviewed by the pharmacist on duty that day for accuracy.

Every day, the pharmacist was required to sign, and the log is required to be kept for a minimum of 2 years. This is a simple format and can be like this:

The undersigned pharmacist hereby attests that all prescription information entered on the date indicated has been reviewed by the pharmacist and is correct.

Date: _____ Shift: _____ to _____

Pharmacist Name (printed): _____

License #: _____

Signature _____

_____

Date: _____ Shift: _____ to _____

Pharmacist Name (printed): _____

License #: _____

Signature _____

_____

Date: _____ Shift: _____ to _____

Pharmacist Name (printed): _____

License #: _____

Signature _____

_____

The **signature logs beginning 12/27/2015 through May 2016** when I began my new position (as I previously indicated) **showed NO SPLIT SHIFTS** as required by the new scheduling **demands by CVS of 3 split shifts per week** to be implemented **November 2015.**

Some **December 2015** dates (Signatures removed for Privacy concerns but, notice the hours of the pharmacist-**full days/NO split shift**):

Date: 12/27/15   Shift: 10 a.m. to 6 p.m.
Date: 12/28/15   Shift: 8 a.m. to 9 p.m.
Date: 12/29/15   Shift: 8 a.m. to 9 p.m.
Date: 12/30/15   Shift: 8 a.m. to 9 p.m.
Date: 12/31/15   Shift: 8 a.m. to 9 p.m.

Some **January 2016** dates (**No split shifts**):

Date: 1/2/16   Shift: 9 a.m. to 6 p.m.
Date: 01/3/16   Shift: 10 a.m. to 9 p.m.
Date: 1/4/16   Shift: 8 a.m. to 9 p.m.
Date: 1/5/16   Shift: 8 a.m. to 9 p.m.
Date: 1/6/16   Shift: 8 a.m. to 9 p.m.

Some **February 2016** dates (**No split shifts**):

Date: 2/1/16   Shift: 8 a.m. to 9 p.m.
Date: 02/3/16   Shift: 8 a.m. to 9 p.m.
Date: 2/4/16   Shift: 8 a.m. to 9 p.m.
Date: 02/09/16   Shift: 8 a.m. to 9 p.m.
Date: 2/10/16   Shift: 8 a.m. to 9 p.m.
Date: 2/11/16   Shift: 9 a.m. to 9 p.m.
Date: 02/22/16   Shift: 8 a.m. to 9 p.m.
Date: 2/23/16   Shift: 8 a.m. to 9 p.m.
Date: 2/25/16   Shift: 8 a.m. to 9 p.m.
Date: 2/26/15   Shift: 8 a.m. to 9 p.m.

Some **March 2016** dates (**No split shifts**):

Date: 03/1/16   Shift: 8 a.m. to 9 p.m.
Date: 03/02/16   Shift: 8 a.m. to 9 p.m.

Date: 03/03/16   Shift: 8 a.m. to 9 p.m.
Date: 03/04/16   Shift: 8 a.m. to 9 p.m.
Date: 03/05/16   Shift: 9 a.m. to 6 p.m.
Date: 03/06/16   Shift: 10 a.m. to 6 p.m.
Date: 03/07/16   Shift: 8 a.m. to 9 p.m.
Date: 03/08/16   Shift: 8 a.m. to 9 p.m.

*This set of signatures/dates revealed that the **Staff Pharmacist** worked 13-hour shifts on **3/2/16, 3/3/16, 3/4/16,** and **3/5/16** (That were supposed to be SPLIT) before working a "short shift" of 9am-6pm followed by a 10am-6pm on a weekend shift. That is followed up by repeated 13-hour shifts on **3/7/16 and 3/8/16.** Pharmacists got NO scheduled breaks with CVS nor LUNCH breaks. **I did not include the signatures for privacy concerns.**

The board of pharmacy has a section concerning the absence of the pharmacist and the rules are as follows:

1140-03-.07 TEMPORARY ABSENCE OF PHARMACIST
A pharmacist is permitted one (1) temporary absence for a period not exceeding one (1) hour per day. During the absence of a pharmacist from the pharmacy practice site, a sign containing the words "pharmacist not on duty" must be conspicuously displayed in the pharmacy practice site. It shall be unlawful to fail or refuse to display the required sign in a conspicuous place when a pharmacist is absent. No medical or prescription order may be compounded or dispensed during the absence of a pharmacist. Additionally, during the absence of the pharmacist the prescription department shall be closed off by physical barrier from floor to ceiling.

The "permitted one (1) temporary absence for a period not exceeding one (1) hour per day" as outlined by the board of pharmacy was NEVER ALLOWED or included in the SCHEDULE for the PHARMACIST in my district. I want the public to know how poorly some management at

CVS has treated their pharmacists with ZERO reprimand. Almost any pharmacist will tell you there is NO PHARMACIST SHORTAGE. Pharmacists are just now REFUSING to work under such conditions. I will share one story that I received while working on documenting the treatment I received over the last several years BY CVS representatives, then I will continue to make my case of Age discrimination, Gender discrimination and possibly even Race (my supervisor was from India and the culture was not female friendly. I will let the reader be the judge on that).

When contacted by the New York Times reporter, Ellen Gabler, who wrote an article on the working conditions for pharmacists and patient safety I was sent this:

"I worked for CVS. They fired me for walking outside to grab a bite of food and fresh air for 6 MINUTES during my 12-hour shift while I was 7 months pregnant. They fired me two months later the week I was going on maternity leave. Cancelled my insurance that night at midnight. I started having contractions early and contracted shingles as a result of the stress of being unemployed and unpaid while having my baby. For 6 minutes of leaving the pharmacy."

The worst part is that this pharmacist was apologetic about leaving the pharmacy unattended for such a short time saying:

I know I broke the law. I don't dispute that. My issue is how they waited until 1 shift before my maternity leave over an incident that happened 2 months prior. Also, you're telling me they have fired every single pharmacist that ever went to their car. Walked out of the building? Smoked a cigarette? (Of course, I wasn't smoking, I was pregnant and wanted some soup for lunch).

I have emails proving the treatment for much worse offenses by men were NOT handled the same way in my district.

> When were you terminated? I
> have e-mails to my supervisor
> where 2 different men floaters
> left the pharmacy unlocked
> (unsecured) after their shift
> and I had to go close the
> pharmacy. They were not
> reprimanded in any way.

I thought I may be able to supply those emails to help her, but she did not pursue any legal action against an almost impossible win. She summed up what we all know (as pharmacists) and this is what THEY call a PHARMACIST SHORTAGE.

> That's a perfect way to
> describe my situation. It's like
> they have a folder of fireable
> offenses for every
> pharmacist, but they only use
> them when it is convenient for
> them. Like when you make too
> much money, when you cause
> waves, when you aren't quick
> enough, etc.

This is so tragic and heartbreaking. The level of cruelty has no name. This is not the only story JUST LIKE THIS!

April and May shifts continued as the previous shifts and revealed NO SPLIT SHIFTS. When I began my shifts at store 7246-Newport (the new location I was forced to transfer to because of performance issues) the current pharmacist and I continued to schedule as the two younger men had done since December of 2015 as shown on the previous pages.

We continued to work the schedule until **I became the target of another manufactured crisis, seemingly by Rush.** He began to heavily focus on the scheduling and it became the center of attention, never mind it was fine for at least the time period beginning in December 2015 through the time I began working store 7246 (the same schedule the younger men had worked).

There were **still exceptions - just not for me.** When I was on vacation, it was permitted for a younger pharmacist from another store, Charlene, to cover shifts outside of the mandatory guidelines of "split 3 days per week." It was also on one of these shifts that Charlene shorted a patient of her pain medications that created additional work for me. I reported it to Rush, but never got a response (see previous test messages to Rush).

Date: 08/30/16   Shift: 8 a.m. to 9 p.m.
Date: 08/31/16   Shift: 8 a.m. to 9 p.m.
Date: 09/02/16   Shift: 8 a.m. to 9 p.m.

Charlene was a (younger) pharmacy manager in another store who often picked up additional shifts. **If the mandatory scheduling was enforced equally in all locations**, Charlene would not have been able to cover my store Monday (4pm-9pm), Tuesday (8am-9pm), Wednesday (8am-9pm) and Friday (8am-9pm) and keep her own store compliant. There are only 7 days in a week so if Charlene spent Tuesday, Wednesday, and Friday at 7246, that would mean only 4 days remained to be SPLIT per MANDATORY GUIDELINES. Saturday and Sunday were short days and were never split therefore, only 2 days remained to SPLIT. She was also in violation of the long days back-to-back on Tuesday and Wednesday, but Charlene wasn't the one who made the schedule. The floater schedules were made by the district scheduler from her district office in Knoxville that sat directly across from Rush- the pharmacy supervisor. The picture painted here points to age discrimination, harassment (possibly) and gender discrimination. There was **no micro-managing or scrutiny until it became, what felt like, a target on my back by Rush**.

The scheduling, as previously stated in my opinion, was something Rush thought he could sink his teeth into. He began directing Marge Ellen (district scheduler for pharmacists) to contact me about the scheduling. Marge Ellen had all the set pharmacy managers and staff pharmacist's schedules for each store at least **a month in advance** so there should have been no problem figuring out when I was at work but there was (or was there)?

I was contacted on my vacation days, days off, and even before my shift non-stop about scheduling compliance. Early **September 2016** was filled with text messages to me from Marge Ellen on behalf of Rush. I will include only a few:

> They said we have to split but nothing definitive from Jefferson. I talked to him and he was supposed to e-mail me but didn't.

Rush wants 3 split days with this new RPh coming

> I can put something in this weekend. What is the best time to start—the week of the 11th?

Probably I have that week covered but yes start splitting that week send me a new schedule will redo if covering with floaters

> Ok, I will try to come up with something

Fri, Sep 2, 12:06 PM

Rush needs you to come in the office Tuesday between 10-3 let me know what time you can come in please

> In Denver- will let you know

Rush, was once again, having Marge Ellen contact me (while **in the Denver airport** on my way back from getting my **son** moved in for **college**) about **scheduling as if it were a** MAJOR STATE/FEDERAL **violation**. While I was in the Denver airport, I spoke with my husband on the phone. He told me he thought he was getting an eye infection, so I instructed him to go to a walk-in clinic before he picked me up.

When I landed, he informed me that the clinic was sending him to an eye specialist IMMEDIATELY. We went directly to Dr. Steven L. Sterling's office (he was staying over to see my husband because of the referral from the walk-in clinic). The infection was so bad, Dr. Sterling wrote for special compounded eye drops to be used on an alternating schedule every hour ATC (around the clock). He called the compounding pharmacy, and they were waiting on us.

The eye **appointments** went from touchdown on **September 2, 2016**, through at least **September 23, 2016**. Most appointments were just a day or two apart. I managed to keep some of the appointment cards and will insert them. The appointments were necessary due to the severity of the infection-the cause, a raindrop that entered the car through a partially rolled down window. The appointments were as frequent as the demands from Rush to come to the district office for a meeting over scheduling. I declined the invitations and chose my family's health (husbands' eyesight) over his frivolous targeted attacks. I was getting very little sleep, and my nerves were beginning to fray. The attacks were taking a toll. Rush did not appear to be leading with heart as the CVS slogan suggests, it was more like he was heartless.

Steven L. Sterling, M.D., P.C.
2607 Kingston Pike Suite 182
Knoxville, TN 37919
(865) 540-1777

For: Robert Payne   Date: 9/6/16

Address:

℞ Tobramycin ophth ointment
Sig: apply to Oס gtts

Dr wanted to Start this AFTER 2 ROUNDS of compounded eye Drops.

Dispense 9 - 1 - 2 - 3 - 4 PRN

☐ No Substitutes unless advised

Steven L. Sterling, M.D., P.C.
2607 Kingston Pike, Suite 182
Knoxville, TN 37919
(865) 540-1777

Robert Payne

has an appointment for

Day Fri Date 9/9 Year 2016 Time 9:00

Steven L. Sterling, M.D., P.C.
2607 Kingston Pike, Suite 182
Knoxville, TN 37919
(865) 540-1777

Robert Payne

has an appointment for

Day Tues Date 9/13 Year 2016 Time 9:30

Steven L. Sterling, M.D., P.C.
2607 Kingston Pike, Suite 182
Knoxville, TN 37919
(865) 540-1777

Robert Payne

has an appointment for

Day MON Date 9-19 Year 2016 Time 3:20

Steven L. Sterling, M.D., P.C.
2607 Kingston Pike, Suite 182
Knoxville, TN 37919
(865) 540-1777

Robert Payne

has an appointment for

Day Fri Date 9/23 Year 2016 Time 2:00

I was not sure why I was receiving text messages on September 2 about scheduling since I had already sent in the month of September on August 2, and it was compliant. I just did not have the names of the other floater pharmacists to include.

September 2016

Sunday	Monday	Tuesday	Wednesday	Thursday	Friday	Saturday

Cancel the 12th as a Vacation Day! I will work.

Complying with the 2 weeks advance scheduling rule.

September 21: My schedule was 8am-2pm and was turned in on the primary schedule **8/2/2016.** No consideration was ever given of the day or time as demonstrated once again in this text by choosing Friday, September 23, 2016, which was my scheduled DAY OFF or Monday when I was scheduled to go in at 4pm and close-but maybe it was.

Wed. Sep 21, 3:29 PM

Rush told me now you hAve to
come in Friday sometime or
Monday give me a time

I was working Wednesday, September 21, 2016, from 8 AM TO 2 PM and a **simple phone call could have been placed while I was on CVS time** rather than a **text on my time** demanding that I come to the district warehouse for a meeting about something I was already compliant with. **CVS did not OWN ME**, but this would make one believe **they thought they did**. This was pure harassment, and I must have been living in Rush's head rent free. My shift ended at 2 PM but the text was not made until 3:29 PM that day.

The text on Monday, September 26, 2016, was made at 8:50am with a sense of **urgency!!!** Rush wanted me **"Off the bench"** . . . effectively firing me or at a minimum, put on temporary leave over a matter that I was compliant with- scheduling. My shift did not start until 4:00PM and it took approximately an hour to drive to the store, but I was expected to go to the district office?

Mon, Sep 26, 8:50 AM

Need to call me!!! Rush wants you off bench till you come in and talk to him.

Just text him and set up a time

Mon, Sep 26, 11:09 AM

I just got up. Have been sick all night. I don't know, but I think it is my nerves. Have had diarrhea and vomiting again!! Trying to get better before I have to be at work by 4 but I guess I shouldn't worry about that now since he doesn't want me on the bench. I am in no shape right now to drive out there.

Text him and let him know he's wanting a time you will come in

September 26, 2016, continued:

It will have to be the week of October 9th since you are on vacation next week

Let me know this week what day during that week you can come in

> Just left urgent care—can't make it in for my shift tonight. I have a doctors excuse if you need it. I am so sorry. I will make it up to you and when I feel better, I will let Rush know when I can be in. Apologize for me. Thank you so much.

Can't do till the week of sept 9th since you are on vacation

Are you going in today

> No

Are you any better

> A little

> Does that mean I can't work until the week of October 9th???

No

You work this week on vacation next week set a meeting with Rush the week of October 9th up

I thought I couldn't work according to him??? I am really confused and this is stressing me out. HELP

You are working this week on vacation next week set a meeting with Rush the week of October 9th up

Did he change his mind? So I can work?

Yes you can work

Thank god! I couldn't pay my bills otherwise.

Delivered

Did you did a new schedule

??? No, it is already in with split shifts. We talked about changing it a little to help Stephanie out since Rush gave her a schedule at her interview.

Do you know what I'm to cover next week since it would be her all night week

She has a schedule Rush gave her, It might be helpful for you to call her?

She wants to make sure you are in agreement with the schedule

Rush gave Steph a "schedule" during her interview without consulting me, the Pharmacy Manager. The conversation was always centered around scheduling. It was fueled by promises Rush made to Stephanie when hiring. It is never right for a pharmacy supervisor to promise and handwrite a schedule for a new hire without consulting the pharmacy manager first, but it happened. The back and forth on scheduling continued and eventually even involved the store manager; again, this was **unprecedented**.

> Anything-have changed the schedule so many times and so has Janie to accommodate the whiner. I don't even know

A response to Marge Ellen from me.

Another attempt to get me to come into the district office (on my time off) to discuss something that was simply not a problem would rear its ugly head. Again, I chose my family's health over the multiple invitations.

Need to set up an appt with Rush. I believe this is about a schedule. Let me know what day you can come in this week. I will need to know what I'm covering next week if you are going to be out

OK - - filling out paperwork now. Will let you know. I told Stephanie she could be Pharmacy Manager and I will float but she doesn't want that cry baby

She just had 4 & 1/2 days off - I get nothing

I was being asked to set up an appointment with Rush even though **I was preparing to take my son to the Mayo Clinic for health concerns.** The **harassment never stopped under any circumstances** and the **turmoil** created by Rush and Stephanie (younger, newly hired pharmacist that Rush promised a schedule to) over the schedule **did not either.**

Oct 7, 2016 at 9:54 PM

I hate to message you this late but we forgot to talk about schedule.
Can we do the schedule example that Rush gave me in my interview? can't work 9 days in a row right now. I'm sorry. I tried.
Thanks
Steph

Still discussing scheduling October 11, 2016. Steph was always contacting me concerning ANOTHER NEW VERSION OF THE SCHEDULES (always saying "I hate to message you"):

Look at schedule Janie did this morning
I'll try it if you want and if it don't work
well try smtg else
If that's ok with you

Oct. 29, 2016, at 6:00 PM

I hate to message you with
everything you have going on.
But I found out thru Marge
Ellen that I still don't have any
vac.
I hate to ask but she told me
to ask you. If your kids aren't
tricking treating Monday
would you want to trade
shifts ?

> I will work all day Monday if
> you work all day Friday

Yes I will. Thank you !!!
I'm sorry to ask you. I was
just going to tk vac bc I know
you have a lot going on with
your son and I hated to ask
but I don't have any to tk still
Marge Ellen said.

In late September/Early October, I worked with Steph and adjusted the schedule to meet her needs when she initially started working as Staff pharmacist at 7246 so she could have 4 & ½ days off. I believed her when she said Rush promised her vacation time, but **his** failed promises did not make me the villain. Here we are still asking for favors (which I AGAIN granted).

Stephanie

Nov 3, 2016 at 3 53 PM

Do you want me to send what she gave us ???

Yes- we can switch if we need to. I haven't really studied it to close

I'll send it the way she sent it Then you can look at it while your off if you want me to do that

Thats fine

Nov 4, 2016, at 8:55 AM

I just wanted to double check You did tell me tues nov 15 that you could not split shift any to where you could go with your son then I could go with my family bc your son has meeting after school

I'm faxing these schedules to Marge Ellen and I just put a question mark on the 15

I gave up trying to know my schedule with any advance knowledge and it came down to me texting and asking:

Mon, Nov 7, 2016, at 11 06 AM

What do I work tomorrow?

Tomorrow is 8-9

Thanks

The scheduling dilemmas were never ending with Steph:

Nov 9, 2016 at 12:28 PM

Do you have plans ?
Would you be able to leave
today at 3 instead if 3 and
then come in Friday at 3
instead of 2 ?
My dads here and we're
waiting on a realtor and she's
ran late
If not it's ok I'll leave and
come on in

November 9, 2016, Steph Elm needed me to make changes to my scheduled shift to accommodate her AGAIN. She would soon (tomorrow, **November 10**, 2016) **make accusations against** me in a secret visit that occurred at the store. Now that the scheduling crisis was run into the ground with no basis for noncompliant claims, let's call a "Code Red" meeting without any explanation.

Code Red

*E*nter Jefferson Gates (District manager)
November 15, 2016, 3:26pm

Jefferson

Nov 15, 2016, at 3:26 PM

After having time to think about our conversation yesterday on the phone, I have checked my personal schedule and it would be more convenient for me to take the second option of meeting with you on Friday. I know you said it would only take 30 minutes of my time to discuss the 2 outstanding issues at 7246 but it is in my opinion that I will be put under undue mental stress which would interfere with my ability to perform my job n a safe clear manner for my patients. It is with this in mind that I choose to meet Friday AFTER my shift. I know you were offering to send a floater in to cover me so as not to impose on my personal time as in the past and for that I thank you. I am assuming that I would not be docked for not being at work at 2 as you requested so I am not sure how you would like to handle Friday. Let me know at your convenience. Thank you.
DaOnda

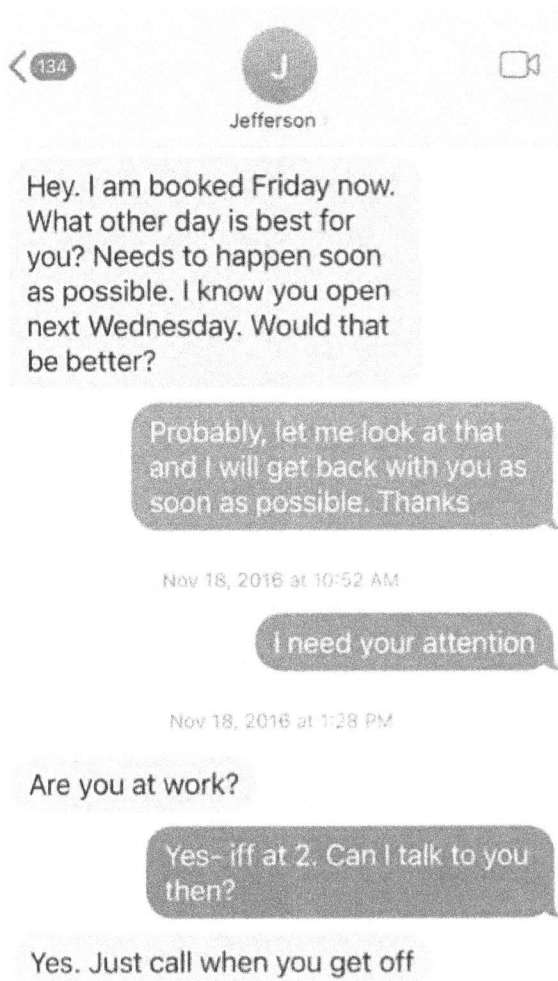

Hey. I am booked Friday now. What other day is best for you? Needs to happen soon as possible. I know you open next Wednesday. Would that be better?

Probably, let me look at that and I will get back with you as soon as possible. Thanks

Nov 18, 2016 at 10:52 AM

I need your attention

Nov 18, 2016 at 1:28 PM

Are you at work?

Yes- iff at 2. Can I talk to you then?

Yes. Just call when you get off

November 16, 2016

I arrived at the district offices on Parkside Drive in Knoxville to meet with Jefferson Gates and was (once again) ambushed with two people other than myself attending the meeting-one as a witness, I suppose. I was not afforded the opportunity to have anyone except myself to stand up for me or be there as an impartial witness. Stef. T. (Another Pharmacist, newly promoted Supervisor, and an ex-partner of mine at 7246) was in attendance for Jefferson.

My gut feelings from prior conversations with Jefferson were playing out- ambush! And were never in my favor. I sat down and Jefferson proceeded to let me know there were some concerns at 7246. I assumed they were targeting me, and I came somewhat prepared to defend myself if I could. Jefferson then took out some papers and began to read **some** statements that were made by my current staff at 7246. I was never allowed to **SEE** the papers, nor was I given names. I was informed that he would be **reading random statements** to **protect the identity** of the person making the statements. Jefferson finished reading **what he felt was important** I suppose and then said he wanted me to answer some questions that he had written down. I agreed to do my best and at the closing of the meeting, I demanded a copy of the questions and answers BEFORE I left. The questions and answers are as follows:

G: After reading you all of the specific allegations toward you what is your take/statement on the situation?

A:

I agree the Pharmacy is a hostile environment. I cannot effectively enforce any CVS Policies/Procedures with a group who has learned over the years to call others about anything that they disagree with. I know better than to call anyone names and threaten physical harm. It is demeaning to me that these allegations could be considered to be true. Jacqueline Myers, store manager, can verify the collusion in the pharmacy. They threaten each other all the time, at this point, a logical person could not take it seriously. This store needs to work as One as in the past, Not a divided nation. The facebook posts and texts should reflect the character. As far as trying to run any pharmacist off, that couldn't be further from the truth. I have offered the pharmacy manager position to Stephanie but she declined. This store has developed this aura over time — it is nothing I have created. I just stepped into it.

11/14/14

Q: Why do you feel that these allegations are being made about you?

A: These allegations are made about me (untrue) to divert the attention from where it should be focused. It is always easier to blame someone else rather than blame yourself and try to change. Human nature — People resist change.

Q: Are there any other comments that you would like to add or anything else you would like to mention around this situation?

A: Not at this time.

Q: During this conversation/investigation how did you feel? Was it handled professionally?
This conversation was handled in a professional manner

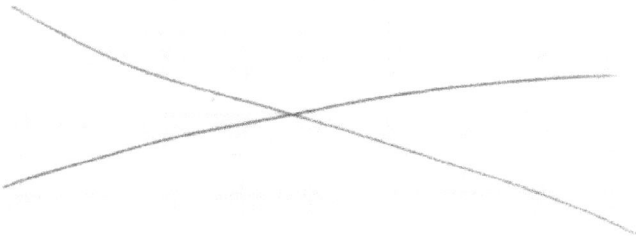

I presented Jefferson with a couple of Facebook posts from some of the staff to show what I thought was happening and how **the hostile working environment was NOT due to me.** The posts were mainly from Charlotte Oli and were directed at other employees. I was only aware of this because the other girls showed me and told me to look at Charlotte's Facebook posts.

I was blindsided again and was not given an opportunity to schedule a time for me to bring my FULL DEFENSE! I was given **page 12** of the employee handbook and told there was a **ZERO TOLERANCE FOR RETALIATION** and sent back to the store. Was I essentially GUILTY without the right to a defense?

That's how CVS conducted that investigation. **It looked like, "If you write what we need to support our narrative, then we will overlook everything you have said and done."**

I was now essentially stripped of any tools I may have had as a pharmacy manager to guide the store and remain compliant. I could not use any sort of **write ups** for inappropriate behavior or negligence of duty without those involved banding together to distort and manipulate corrective action plans and call them **RETALIATION**. I was sent into the proverbial lion's den and not only was it a dangerous situation for me, ultimately it was a danger to the public whom we were there to serve. In no way did this fit the code red narrative.

If given the opportunity, I would have presented the following for each technician and Stephanie; however, I was never given the opportunity so I will present some of my evidence in this format:

Deb Kelner

Aug 23, 2016, 2:44 PM

I know you are off but Tessa said I had to ask you Iam down to work Labor Day I work July 4 it isn't my turn to work I had plan to go to the camping ground where my family is going camping Charlotte hadn't work one yet at all this year can you fix this please

Fix it -- I asked her if she asked for volunteers. She seems to always be off early etc. I don't really care who works so let Darren look at it and make it fair.

If I do have to work it she can work New Year day

I am mad at you anyway!!! lol!!

Butt head !!!

Delivered

You love me

No!

Yes you do lol

No! No! No! 🤍🤍🤍

Lol

🥺

You at work?

Following is another conversation (Debbie contacting me on my day off AND while I was in Las Vegas because I was always there for them and told them they could contact me).

Sep 1, 2016, 10:17 AM

Can Janet do a partial on OxyContin he is a customer of our and all we have is 49 and put label to the side until it comes in

She is making a wish list for the company

it has to be completed within 72 hours—that is the law

He can take what we have, and the Dr can write a new rx for the rest

Option

Otherwise—illegal

Then we will give it back

Ok

They shouldn't have terminated ir whatever they did to Darren

I know they're no. Need for me to come in Monday no cII lol

I will place an order this weekend, but it won't be there until Tuesday at best

What?

Oh

I am a little slow this morning

Debbie was kidding and said there was no need to come into work Monday because there was no Pharmacist on duty while I was out of town that could legally place a Schedule II Narcotic order so we would not have any narcotics to sell. This would not have been a problem if CVS had not terminated Darren, (my partner) while I was gone.

That ok Iam too

Still early here

3 hours behind you

Sorry you can kill me later

I don't do mornings anyway

Ok-deal

I need you for now !! Lol

I will not Ted n more go back to bed

(She meant "I will not text anymore, go back to bed"). I was in Las Vegas moving my son into college and she was texting me at 10:17am in TN.

This conversation is important for several reasons. First, it shows that Debbie knew she could contact me anytime she had concerns. Second, it shows that Debbie looked out for the store to the best of her ability-she had a good heart. Third, Debbie and I could kid with each other, as is clear by her statement:

"**Sorry, you can kill me later**" and my response of "**OK- deal.**" This will be important on November 10, 2016, during the secret meeting with CVS.

Cant now

I havent slept much in the last week

Talk later got to get back to work

Leave here at 5:45am tomorrow—

Delivered

Ok

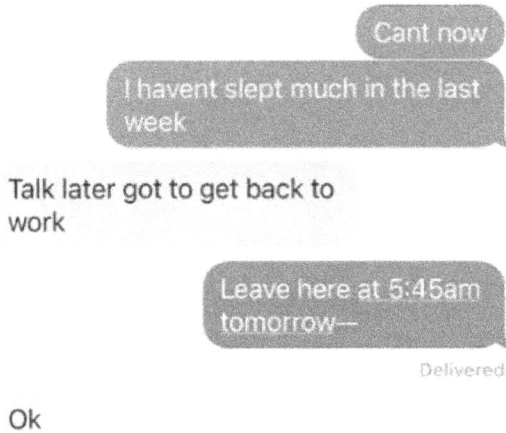

Knowing that Debbie often reached out to me when I was not at work, I had no reason to believe that she would have been one of the employees who wrote complaints about me. **I would find out the truth, two years later.**

Next up: Amelia

I had known Amelia for quite some time. Amelia was always willing to help and was very talkative and engaged with the patients every chance she had. Her former employer and friend of mine used to call her an empty wagon—"She was always rattling." It was an ongoing inside joke that we could laugh about and break the monotony at work. While I was Pharmacy Manager at store #3743, Amelia asked me to help her get a job at CVS. I was a reference for Amelia, and she gained employment with the company. Amelia began working with CVS in Greeneville prior to transferring to Newport. I never imagined we would be working together but it was nice to have another familiar face around and who was strong in their roles. I was convinced that Amelia was not one of the employees who took a part in this witch hunt. It's amazing what a human will say when coaxed, put on a pedestal, and made to feel like the most important person in the room. **I would find out the truth two years later.**

Text Message
Jun 8, 2016 at 10:13 PM
Ok. Thanks for offering to stay late
No problem.
You 2 were awesome tonight- I really appreciate you
Thank you! It's good to be appreciated
I know, and I try to tell you. You guys are truly way better than what I had!
I'm glad that you have a team that will mostly work together now.

It really is nice. I don't expect to get along all the time but most of the time is very nice

You'll get everyone on the same page. I have faith.

I hope because I know you guys can be number 1. You have the combined talent

Exactly. Especially if we have a pharmacist that is working with us.

I know you all have your own talents and I trust you to do your jobs. I am not going to hold anyone back. I am there to help

We finally have someone who sees our strengths and allows us to use them to the fullest.

Please, please, don't send me Newport!

You and I both have worked in different pharmacy settings. Good and bad.

True

Guess that's why we can see better ways to get things done. And think outside of the box.

Yep

I had just complimented Amelia and Charlotte on how nice it was to work with the two of them. They worked well as a team, and it was an enjoyable shift.

> She and I have been the ones that have been closing together most nights since she started. I give her as much training and benefit of my experience as I can.

> She is doing really well for being new

> I think so too. Others won't give her any slack and get upset when she asks questions.

> She doesn't ask that many questions

> Besides- that is how you learn

> Exactly. The others ask me more questions about stuff that they SHOULD know after all of the years that they have been doing this.

> Amen!

Amelia was equivalent to a watch dog for me. She let me know everything going on at the store when I was not present. Sometimes, she let her imagination run away with her, but I often took it with a grain of salt. I appreciated her efforts and put her actions in perspective. She, like most individuals, liked to feel like they were playing a key role-it gave her a sense of pride as seen in the following conversations (**while I was not on duty**).

Jun 17, 2016, at 7:52 AM

Darren just let a customer in the store and they are in there alone.

Aug 23, 2016, at 8:59 AM

No word about what Rush is going to do? I hope nothing even under the circumstances

I think its OK. He said that it was

Aug 26, 2016, at 8:49 PM

=8??Sunday is Darren's last day. He talked them into letting him resign instead of being fired. Not sure who we will get in his place. Just wanted you to know

=8??what you were coming back into.

There was an incident involving "metrics" and how they were met. Apparently, Darren was so desperate to "meet" the target set by corporate that he got a little creative. I was not privy to what happened, and it all took me by surprise. The next conversation is concerning what took place. Amelia once again informed me.

Yeah.

They are so heartless

DaOnda

Yes. I hope the snitch is proud of herself.

Amelia

Someone had to go to them--- they asked me but I told them I didn't know because i hadn't worked on his shift. Anything I could say would be merely "hear say".

Yep. Lead was acting guilty as all get out today.

Well – there you go?

The whole thing is not worth him losing his job. What about Chapman Highway and the Extra Care cards???

Or Stan sleeping on the job.

Oh yeah, maybe I will text that to them. I have the picture

Please?? I don't know that we can handle having him back. People will most likely quit.

Sep 22, 2016, at 4:27 PM

Charlotte and I have the perfect lead tech candidate for you

?????

Lindsey

She doesn't do anything but play with paperwork. U will never know the difference

I'm ready to wring her neck. We are busting our butts and she I'd filing papers.

She doesn't care. She goes home at 5. I'm at lunch or i wouldn't be texting.

Stephanie told her to come back and count while I'm at lunch.

No change in pace

Things would begin to change in the relationships between the staff. I noticed a lot of animosity and disrespect and managing became almost impossible.

Sep 22, 2016, at 7:15 PM

Do not schedule me to work with Charlotte again. Sick of her screaming attitude.

And threats.

Just get along! It is hard enough on everyone, CVS is stressing us all out! We all are feeling the pressure and it is affecting how we treat each other.

OK. I will not be screamed at again.

Breathe

Every time I try to explain something she doesn't understand I catch hell. She can leave at 8 as scheduled and she is threatening.

Just get along, it cant be that hard.

Charlotte was the newest employee and I had never worked with her before.

She seemed very nice and respectful and eager to learn. Tressa, the lead pharmacy technician, had been given the scheduling assignment by Darren. It seemed that Amelia and Charlotte were often scheduled together and on the closing shift. All was well at first (as seen in the previous conversation) but as time went on, Charlotte and Amelia began to develop an unhealthy work relationship. I tried to smooth things over the best I could, but sometimes it was out of my control.

I did not realize for some time that the new pharmacist was causing division between me and the rest of the staff. They would tell me how she brought in cupcakes, etc. That was a nice gesture until my eyes were forced open by other technicians and the fact that the pharmacist was manipulating scenarios to her benefit.

I began noticing a lot of inaccuracies in the inventory and many were controlled substances. I reported all of my findings the moment they were noticed. I was instructed by Loss Prevention to initiate reports during the cycle counts of each item I found to be of concern. This would get more frequent and include more items as time went on. I did not know who to trust at this point and the chaos at the store increased.

Multiple pharmacy technicians began alerting me to posts on Facebook that Charlotte was making and said they were about Amelia. In my mind, the posts could not be a coincidence after Amelia returned from vacation and the animosity between the two was on the rise. Some of the posts follow and will be relevant in two years.

Charlotte wrote on her Facebook: (spelling and grammar as originally posted on all following texts)

August 25, 2016
You know I really feel sorry for people that have to tell everyone about their life. Cause as I watch them tell the story all happy, I can see on the other persons face that they just want them to shut up. It's even worse when the person tried to walk away, and he or she is still telling the story like someone cares. If we wanted to know about ur life we would ask until then keep it to ur self.

Deb Kelner "liked" this post.

Charlotte also posted:

October 26 at 6:13 PM-Newport
U ever hear someone talk so much u want to tell them to shut up nobody cares about what they say? Yeah im almost to that point. im fixin to hurt somebodys feelings

..and another post:

October 26 at 5:52 pm
U know when that person goes on a vacation and it is the greatest days of ur life and then they come back and everyone is like omg they are back here we go back to bein in hell. Yeah that happened this week. To bad that didnt take a permanent vacation.

Amelia was on vacation the previous week and just returned.

. . . AND ANOTHER POST (spellings remain as posted):

October 31 AT 2:09 PM
Im so sick and tired of people running their mouth about me. if u have something to say about me then say it to my face if u can't then keep ur cowardly bitch ass mouth shut. Cause i promise u when i catch u out i am gonna beat the brakes off ur ass. U aint nothing but a pussy ass bitch. U always have diarrhea of the mouth everything u say smells like ur shitty ass breath. Dont start no shit there wont be no shit but unfortunately u done unleashed the bitch in me. Good luck cause u can't handle me when im like this.

Deb Kelner "liked" this post.

Similar posts continued but the most telling of what was going on was a post featuring an ambulance with lettering on the side that said "Wambulance." It wasn't the post as much as the people who were "tagged" in the post:

Jolene, Deb, and the new pharmacist, Steph. It appeared to show there was now a small "clique" in the pharmacy. The division of the staff was becoming clear. We were no longer ONE TEAM. I could not manage this while being an apparent target by Rush.

The last post by Charlotte that I will share simply said:
Had a great day at work today!!!
The comments under the post revealed more:

Deb: Good!!!
Charlotte (to Deb): Missed u there!!
Jolene: It was because you worked with me and Stephanie.   lol
It seemed that Charlotte, Jolene, Deb, and Steph were becoming quite close. This development was of great concern. **I would find out the truth, two years later.**

Jolene

Jolene was a long-time friend in the pharmacy world. I met Jolene while filling in at another pharmacy, so I knew she was a hard worker. Jolene was super-fast at production (printing and filling prescriptions) but did not like any of the patient facing stations such as data entry, check-out and drive-through. Jolene came to CVS through a buy out of an independent pharmacy and was given a senior status of 13 years 5 months.

I knew I could count on Jolene for honesty because of our background together. Jolene called me while I was at 3743 to ask what to do about a pharmacist who had been secretly drinking a hydrocodone containing cough syrup. I directed her to our Loss prevention department who would follow up on her concerns and take the responsibility for corrective action. I was told, by Jolene, that cameras were put in; the pharmacist was filmed drinking the cough syrup in the back aisle of the pharmacy and corrective action was taken-the pharmacist was charged and terminated. **We worked under MANY CAMERAS.**

I felt comfortable going into store 7246 (Newport) because I had a long history with the girls. I knew they had weaknesses, but I also knew they had the talent to be number one. I just had to assess what was happening with the prior pharmacists and get them to act as a team and focus on the goals.

The lead technician was making the schedule for the pharmacy technician staff. It seemed like she was making the schedule in her favor and not dividing the shifts fairly. I let her continue to make the schedule but tried to act as a liaison between her and the others to get them to learn to work together as a team and solve differences and concerns. The following reveals some conversations that took place between Jolene and me. She was not happy with the scheduling and thought the lead technician was taking advantage of her position. Jolene was not the only one unhappy with how the lead was handling her position, so was Amelia. The two of them were inquiring about becoming the Lead Technician and taking over some of the responsibilities and gaining more authority.

Sep 10, 2016, at 6:48 PM

What do I need to do for lead tech....I've had enough of Amelia thinking she has it already!!!

I have to check the process to see if it has changed. Used to be nothing!!

Lol....ok....I want the job then...

Oct 2, 2016, at 9:51 PM

The schedule needs to be changed...I'm working all closings for the next 2 week ...lindsey...might tech and Peggy can do their share of closings...so can Amelia

I texted Tressa to look at it and swap some shifts to make it fair if you have all closings. Should be shared. I didnt look at it closely. Let me know

And my knees and legs cannot do 10 and 11 he days

Ok...she,want me this week and next week and they are all closings...she needs to go ahead and quit

She is going to look at it- calm down redneck!!! Lol

Lol....ok thanks

Help her look at it

You not working

On vacation

Well shoot....ok have fun

Oct 3, 2016 at 11:19 PM

I know you don't want to hear this but I am now closing 3 weeks solid!!! Tessa has no I tensions of changing any of it...told me to find someone to swap...something should be done about her...im beyond pissed off!

I made myself available to all of them anytime they needed anything. I thought that would be a way to let them try to work things out between themselves, but they knew they could contact me if they needed to. I was in Las Vegas moving my son into college and was talking to my sister. She said some of my employees were harassing her on Facebook. I reached out to Jolene to see what was going on.

Oct 4, 2016 at 5:03 PM

Call me if you are not at work
🖤🖤🖤🖤

Oct 4, 2016 at 6:04 PM

Tell your friend to unblock me
and deb

It is my sister and she was
originally referencing the
other store. You two took it
out of context and we need to
all get along

I thought it was some
smartass from another store
trying to be cute...,had never
heard you talk about her

She thought you guys were
giving me a hard time--- total
misunderstanding

Tell her we thought she was
messing with you being here

I could always count on Jolene and Deb. We were always in touch
and just a phone call or text away. **They were my protectors in a sense
(OR WERE THEY)?**

Nov 8, 2016, at 8:18 AM

Charlotte called in, can you come in early

Im fixing to go vote then I will be on

Thanks

Welcome 😊

Nov 10, 2016 at 5:48 PM

What did your friends ask about today??? Inquiring minds want to know!

About Charlotte and Amelia...i,said yes it was meant about Amelia....everyone knows that....lol

True. Charlotte lied to them

Big time....lol

Anything else

You know how it started don't you

No...I heard Amelia fussing but she,aint,going to confront Charlotte

Amelia told me about Charlotte trying to get everyone to call in on me so I confronted Charlotte and she got mad and said Amelia was lying.......... then that night------ facebook time

Oh ......she never came out and asked,me but I heard that

Nobody asked me but then again, they always come in when I am not there---- strange👀

I like the eyeballs....how did you do that

They are loaded onto my phone with all the other emoji's---- magic!

Little did I know the meetings that were being discussed were not about the hostility occurring between Amelia and Charlotte, they were concerning me. Amelia told me that Charlotte was trying to get everyone in the pharmacy to get together and make an ethics complaint against me to get me fired but she was not going to participate. I thought to myself, after texting Jolene about what was happening, they were going to do to me what they had done to the other pharmacists at this store-file an ethics complaint. Jolene was not forthcoming with this information and changed the subject by asking about the eyeballs emoji on my phone.

I now felt that she was a part of what was happening. They were used to running the store their way and as hard as I would try, it would not change things.

I knew the inventory was out of kilter and I was consumed with the implications of inaccurate quantities, especially with narcotics. They tried to get me to believe that my current partner was taking them, but this could not be true since he was in a recovery network known as PRN-Pharmacist Recovery Network. He often had to go for random drug screenings and had never missed or failed one. This added to my stress and hopelessness that Rush had already bestowed upon me, now I had to worry about my license as well. I was fortunate to have Jolene as a friend- or was I? **I would find out the truth two years later.**

Lindsey

Lindsey was the eldest of the team. I worked with Lindsey as a floater pharmacist at REVCO in Newport when I was a very young pharmacist and in my 20's. I had known Lindsey for over 20 years and was familiar with her capabilities. Lindsey was the type of worker that knew one speed-slow, but she completed each task methodically. I knew Lindsey could not be asked to do more than one thing at a time. She was not a multi-tasker and would push back if asked to do more than she thought she could or should.

Lindsey was usually even tempered but there were times when she was not, like all of us. She had a very stubborn streak and tried to stay out of the drama of the pharmacy for the most part. Lindsey had her opinions, and we would often talk about these in private conversations. We were closer in age than the rest and thought somewhat alike. Although Lindsey was slow, she showed up and did her job to the best of her abilities- good or bad. I was almost certain that Lindsey would not have been a party to the "lets gang up on DaOnda and make an ethics complaint" plan to get me fired. **I would find out the truth two years later.**

Stephanie (new staff pharmacist)

Darren was terminated (to my surprise) while I was on vacation. I was notified by Amelia so I would not be surprised when I returned. She thought it was due to him changing the patients phone number to the time and temperature or something to that effect before calling them so he could make one of the metrics by "reaching" the patient and being on the phone for the required amount of time to get points, but I have never confirmed that. Amelia thought it was the lead technician, Tessa, who had management check the phone number he was using but forgot to change back after each call that revealed what he was doing. Some of the other technicians shared the same with me so it may have been true, I cannot confirm.

When Stephanie arrived, I warned her to watch her back. I knew things were happening but could not say for sure. I thought it would be only fair that she be aware and make her own decisions. Stephanie was promised a schedule from Rush during her interview that she shared with me. This was by no means the usual way incoming pharmacists were placed on the schedule in a store. Schedules were made by the Pharmacy Manager and the incoming pharmacist would assume the position of the departing pharmacist - simple. This would not be the case in this instance, why would it be, I was involved.

I covered the scheduling conflicts previously so I will not cover it again here. I did not get to know Stephanie due to the chaos that was being created by Rush and the staff. I was merely trying to survive and take care of my family issues that I also discussed previously. I tried to give pointers to Stephanie where I could, but I was not willing to give my PERSONAL time and be PHYSICALLY PRESENT. I tried to leave notes to direct her and texted when need be. This would be turned against me later.

Sep 22, 2016, at 9:47 PM

> I hope tonight was bearable. Amelia and Charlotte were in a texting war to me 😊 . I tried to get them to work together but I don't think I was successful.

Sep 23, 2016 at 7:07 PM

Can you call me sometime I need to discuss some things with you going on here

Sep 26, 2016 at 4:24 PM

> Adjust the schedule Rush gave you-- I just want every other Friday, Saturday and Sunday. Sorry I could not make it today

No prob hope you feel better

> Thanks. Let Marge Ellen 'know what it is.

> I am very flexible- just keep Fri, Sat, and Sunday together as days off

Sep 27, 2016 at 10:58 AM

> Did you come up with a schedule?

I was always available to all of my staff, including my staff pharmacist. The following text reveals that **she even texted me on MY TIME OFF** to ask simple questions that everyone on staff should have known. I was very organized and kept all protocols in convenient locations (but **I would be called lazy and not caring about the store later**. I often checked in to see if there were any questions and if the new pharmacist was taught proper procedures. My mind was on work and the processes of work, while Steph was, well her words speak louder (in a following text).

Oct 31, 2016 at 11:28 AM

I'm not going back to him

I was on the phone telling
Teresa to pray for me before I
have a nervous breakdown

Oct 10, 2016 at 1:24 PM

Can you call me at store
Where is zostavsx protocol for
here

Oct 30, 2016 at 12:37 PM

Do you check in CII orders in
the computer under CII
check-in Delivery??

Discrepancies on counts and I
need to know if anyone
showed you???

Nov 6, at 2:46 PM

Check workload and do the
weekly regulatory review.
Also, under MyCustomer
there will probably be PGN
calls to be made-check them.

Nov 6, 2016 at 7:05 PM

I called my friend Michelle
whose pic at cvs in va and she
walked me thru the PGN calls
so I did those.
She said the reg review was
too lengthy for her to explain
cvs policy over the phone and
I need to been shown first
how to do it so I can see
what's expected. She said
she normally goes in 30 min
early so she can explain
things to her partner when
needed. So it still needs
completed.

If reports did not get done, for whatever reason, I would be "held responsible." I knew this from earlier conversations with Rush, so I wasn't taking any chances.

Stephanie often left unfinished work for me. I would begin my shift like this:

Steph Elm was only at store 7246 for approximately 3 months, so I would not think she would have been on board to write anything supporting an ethics complaint to get rid of me. **I would find out the truth two years later.**

I was never given the opportunity to defend myself. Just take page 12 and go back to the store, oh and there is ZERO RETALIATION. CVS Policies outlined how the company "**Investigates all good faith reports of wrongdoing**." That would turn out to be a questionable statement.

As employees, we were given handbooks and guidelines. Included was the following:

Investigations

"**The Company investigates all good-faith reports of wrongdoing. If you are asked to participate in an internal investigation of misconduct or unethical behavior, you are required to cooperate.**"

"**If after investigating any complaint of harassment, prohibited discrimination, or retaliation, CVS Health determines that the complaint was made maliciously or that a colleague has maliciously provided false information regarding the complaint, disciplinary action may be taken against the individual who filed the complaint or who gave the false information.**"

CVS apparently failed to complete all investigation steps. I was never given the names and corresponding statements to be able to defend myself. **Two years later,** I would gain access to the full content of the letters written and the names behind the XXX letters. I returned to the store with page 12 as a reminder that I could not say or do anything, and I would file my own Ethics complaint when appropriate. It did not take long. November 21, I filed my own Ethics complaint. I LEFT OUT THE DETAILS AND NAMES FOR A LATER DATE

Report Details
Report Submission Date 11/21/2016

Reported Company/Branch Information

Location Store-**7246-Newport-7246**
346 COSBY HIGHWAY
City/State/Zip: NEWPORT, TN, 37821, UNITED STATES

Organization/Building name
CVS

Location/Address

Location Store-7246-Newport-7246
346 COSBY HIGHWAY

City
Newport

State/province
Tennessee

Zip/postal code
37821

Country
United States

Is management aware of this problem?
Yes

What is the general nature of this matter?
Possible threat of violence, policy violation, unprofessional behavior

Please provide the specific or approximate time this incident occurred:
Last week

How long do you think this problem has been going on?
One week

How did you become aware of this violation?
It happened to me

Are there any other witnesses?
Yes

The response from corporate concerning my report revealed:

* **Store #169**. That was incorrect. The report I made was for **Store #7246**. This was another example of either inferior record keeping on the part of CVS Health and affiliates or another way to **make things disappear**. CVS Locator reveals store #169 was located in Rockville, MD. **Maybe that is an equivalent to "FILE 13."**

* The investigation was **CLOSED**. ". . . necessary appropriate actions have been taken." ALL of the employees involved were still employed and NO DISCIPLINARY ACTIONS appeared to have been taken.

* I emailed asking for the resolution that was taken after logging in with the Report Key to check the progress of the investigation.

Questions and Comments
Answer questions about your report. 11/23/2016 9:37 AM

Please note that this Ethics Line case is under Investigation. Feel free to check back periodically for updates.

What specific actions have been taken? Disciplinary actions? Has the workplace become conducive to allow appropriate pharmacist functions to occur within the state law and CVS policies? Please explain how the matters have been handled to ensure the safety of the public and to protect the pharmacist on duty.

The response I received:

1/20/1017 1:59 PM
Thank you for contacting the Ethics Line with your concerns regarding an employee at store **169**. Be assured that the matters in this report have been brought to the attention of management with need to know and that where necessary appropriate actions have been taken. **This investigation is now closed.**

NO RESPONSE WAS EVER GIVEN!

My complaint detailed what was occurring at the store. I included one example of Jolene bypassing a prompt at the drive-thru window that mandated she call the pharmacist (me) over to counsel the patient on a NEW prescription. When the incident happened, I did a **screen shot** of the **date, time, and the drive-thru location**. When I asked Jolene about what had happened, she replied **"I went through it quicker than I thought."** I asked her to sign the screenshot and she replied: **"I ain't signing shit"** (11/18/2016 at 10:49 AM). It appeared that she intentionally bypassed a MANDATORY CVS policy and caused me to be in violation of both the CVS POLICY AND THE STATE BOARD OF PHARMACY BOARD RULES on patient counseling that I previously covered. I was under a ZERO TOLERANCE of retaliation and harassment, so I used the Ethics Line to file the complaint along with other instances of the same behavior by Charlotte.

I thought this was the safest way to proceed without a conspiracy being brought against me for retaliation and harassment. I would let the Ethics line start an investigation and it would be properly documented by an impartial OUTSIDE SOURCE. I was wrong. Nothing appeared to have been investigated, and **CVS Counsel defended the actions later**. I tried to explain how the technicians had been "running" the store previously in deposition, but it seemed to be of little concern and falling on deaf ears for the protection of corporate interests.

Any situation was turned, "spun" to be against me and what I did or did not do wrong. It appeared the technicians were never questioned or "investigated" for making True or False statements and NO DISCIPLINARY actions were taken against them.

He even implied that I left the company before the investigation was completed and therefore, I did not know how it turned out and whether disciplinary actions were taken.

The note mentioned in deposition that was passed to me:

Overheard her tell
Scarlet
She wasn't going
to do
Anything
today

I found that this is how I was treated by a member of CVS management. It appeared the entire time that he was looking for a way to either terminate me or get me to quit on my own. The violations that were committed by the technicians were defended by every level of CVS upper management I dealt with revealing a troublesome portrayal that suggested patient safety is of little concern.

"-and to your knowledge not intentionally failed to do so."

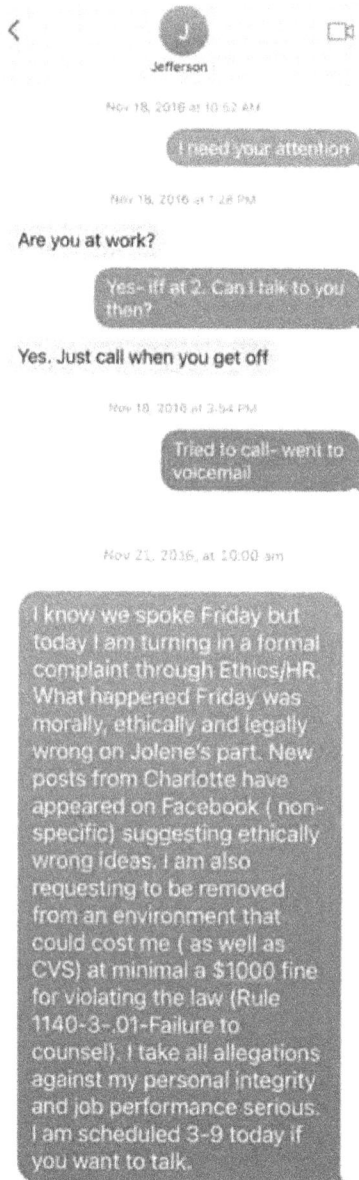

Jefferson

Nov 18, 2016 at 10:52 AM

I need your attention

Nov 18, 2016 at 1:28 PM

Are you at work?

Yes- iff at 2. Can I talk to you then?

Yes. Just call when you get off

Nov 18, 2016 at 3:54 PM

Tried to call- went to voicemail

Nov 21, 2016, at 10:00 am

I know we spoke Friday but today I am turning in a formal complaint through Ethics/HR. What happened Friday was morally, ethically and legally wrong on Jolene's part. New posts from Charlotte have appeared on Facebook (non-specific) suggesting ethically wrong ideas. I am also requesting to be removed from an environment that could cost me (as well as CVS) at minimal a $1000 fine for violating the law (Rule 1140-3-.01-Failure to counsel). I take all allegations against my personal integrity and job performance serious. I am scheduled 3-9 today if you want to talk.

I tried to reach out to Jefferson on November 18, but he was not available. It was getting to be impossible to work at #7246 and I needed to talk to him. Four days later and I could not do it anymore.

The Tipping Point

*A*fter the "Code Red" meeting, the store was no longer manageable and my own well-being as well as patient safety was at risk. I could no longer take what was happening to me and I snapped. I arrived at the store at 8:00am and opened as usual. It wasn't long before Charlene called the store (to a front store employee) to say she would be coming in late, if at all. The message was relayed to me. That was not the procedure to be followed but after the actions of Jefferson at the "code red" meeting and the gift of page 12 with strict instructions of ZERO TOLERANCE FOR RETALIATION, the entire pharmacy staff was entitled to do as they pleased.

They were given immunity from any type of corrective action because that may be misconstrued as RETALIATION. I texted Jefferson because I felt it would be futile to text Rush. He was rarely involved in solutions to any problems I encountered. His only goal seemed to be to get rid of me.

Get me out NOW!!!!! I need to leave before I have a nervous breakdown. Charlotte hasn't shown up--8am shift. Outside regulatory review is here, still have 18 in red from yesterday, waiting bin is stacked from the last 5 days, monthly Rx validation overdue.........

I'll be out there today.

Bring a replacement if I can make it

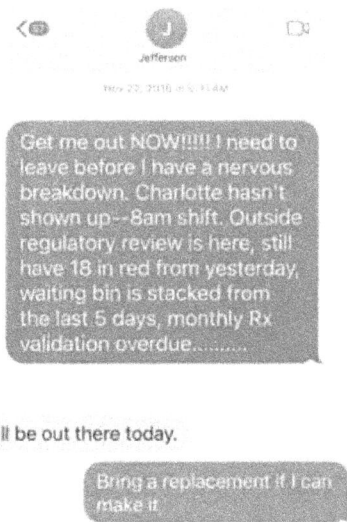

I stayed as long as I could. I felt as though I was not being taken seriously. My mental health was being toyed with, the patients' health was at risk and all I got was "I'll be out there today." Rush was a pharmacist and could have easily stepped in and helped. I closed the pharmacy department and sent Lindsey up front to work so she would not be punished and lose hours. I left the store and went home immediately. My world had just crashed with no support from my immediate supervisors and no one to take the situation seriously. I did not have anyone I felt I could trust.

Jefferson tried to call me, but I could not bring myself to answer my phone. What would I say to change the situation. I was mentally exhausted and all I wanted to do was sleep. I had no options, and I was for sure not going to be secluded with either Rush or Jefferson in a disadvantaged meeting again. I chose to sleep and would address them later.

After waking up, I texted Jefferson since Rush appeared to be less than a positive party to solutions for me. I could not wrap my head around what was going on at the store. All the technicians (except Charlotte) had been long time acquaintances of mine and I considered them friends. They all had their strengths, but I suppose when you are put in a position of power, it goes to your head, and you forget humanity and compassion and can be coerced into just about anything. **I would find out two years later.**

Nov 22, 2016, at 5:20 PM

> Sorry for not answering. I can't hold a good conversation at this time. I didn't want to close today but I felt so overwhelmed emotionally that it wasn't safe for me to try to perform my duties safely. This happened to me and Lindsey last week and it resulted in a misfill of a prescription on the fathers name instead of the son. I don't know how it got through the register and without counsel as it was a 00 - Charlotte rang it up. Stephanie informed me of it yesterday but as the discovering pharmacist, she should have turned it in with details. She gave it to me. No one was harmed, the father apparently brought it back and a refund was given but when waiting on another patient, I found the son's prescription in the bin that I had filled that day as well. Whichever pharmacist works there is in tremendous danger professionally so I had to remove myself from that. When leaving, Lindsey relayed concerns about it as well. You have to do something- they are
> Not innocent and are truly heartless. I thought I could change things but they don't want to change. I hated to leave Janie before- she was defenseless against them. They have the talent combined to perform the job as expected but they also have the will to run the pharmacy the way they have become accustomed to-- their way. If I no longer have a job I understand but at least I have a license in good standing and 3 years in a row of EE (as well as my integrity).

Nov 22, 2016 at 8:41 PM

Can you talk tomorrow? I will reach out to you at your convenience. Not sure when you are scheduled to work?

8a-2p. Not a good idea. I "know" them better than you. It really upsets me about Jolene

They don't do things themselves

The old saying is "If you ain't from there, you don't go there" Newport that is. I have been going there since I was 24, so I know

Are you there in the morning?

Supposed to be

If they do damage to my truck, it is really on

I am more concerned about my license/ fines/ misfilling prescriptions....you know. The " little" things. 😵 CVS owes me a safe environment to work.

I just closed a pharmacy! And all Jefferson appeared to be concerned about was "when you are scheduled to work?" He should have said, "When are you scheduled to work? I will have Rush cover until we find someone else, and we will work through this." This did not happen and,

I believe, was never the intent. This was a situation for Rush, but where was he? Apparently, nowhere to be seen.

The last conversation with Jefferson was November 22, 2016, at 3:08pm. He was trying to come up with a solution at this point. He was going to have Rush cover me and set up a time to talk.

> So do you want Rush to cover the shift and you call Marge Ellen and pick up a shift to offset it?

> It is so late in the week and I am on this weekend so I will work it against my better judgement.

> It's your call. Just let me know. If you change your mind let me know as soon as you can.

> Cover me. Make me a floater?

> I'll have rush cover you tomorrow. Call me tomorrow at your convenience.

> Ok

November 23, 2016, 9:26AM came with an unexpected call, it was Rush. He spent **less than one minute** and influenced what would happen to me for the next **five years of my life.** I was expecting him to discuss covering my shift, but instead, he told me I could not come back until released by a physician as if I had done something wrong. Still no mention of addressing my concerns in the Ethics complaint.

+1 (865) 692-5087

Knoxville, TN

message   call

November 23, 2016

9:26 AM   Incoming Call   1 minute

I had no "physician" or a need for one, so I chose to call the employee assistance program (EAP) called Lifescope. I was given a choice of "Physicians/Counselors," so I chose one from the options given by the agent.

By 9:53AM on November 23,2016, I had followed the directions Rush had given me.

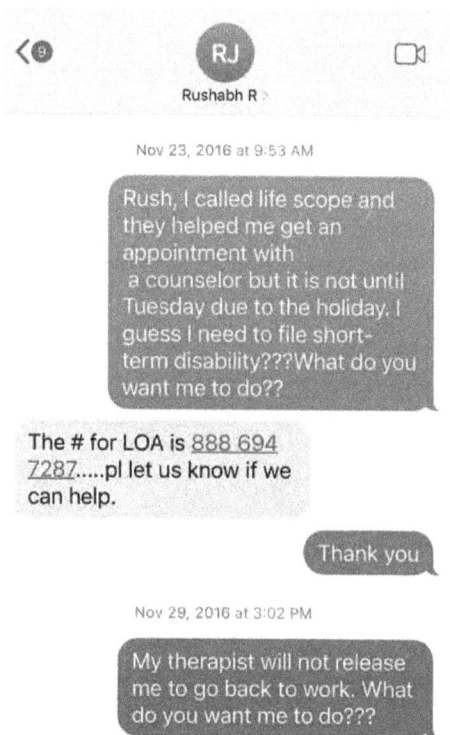

I would be accused of planning what happened then and what would happen. I was forced by Rush to see a doctor, or I could not return. His instructions were to call Lifescope, or a doctor and I was told I could not return until I was released. **Rush FORCED ME OUT OF WORK AND TOLD ME TO FILE FOR LOA VIA TEXT.** I was now without work and money, and it was almost Thanksgiving. I was wondering, what did I have to be thankful for? I was devastated and I was supposed to file for Leave of Absence according to Rush. I had never had such a feeling in my life, but this trauma was the beginning of my growth emotionally from the ground up and one day make a difference as a healthcare professional if I could survive.

Dec 22, 2016, at 11:46 AM

I know you have other things on your plate besides me; however, since my next appt. with therapist given by lifescope isn't until Thursday next week, I requested an extension on the LOA you suggested. Short-term disability is declining due to work related issue now I need to file workers comp . Do I call 1-888-694-7287 (I found it under myHR)? I also have the screen print with the date/ time, etc that Jolene violated (thus causing me to be in violation if the state law not to mention CVS policy) with the exact response given by her and Amanda signed as a witness. I also have a print if the nasty comments made by Charlotte on facebook. I wanted to send this to you to look at first. I can call you if convenient.

By 10:14AM, Rush would call me and spend an entire 3 minutes of his time telling **me to** call and **file** workers compensation. That was what I did. He never addressed my concerns I texted to him. He was directing my actions and once again, I would be accused of willfully taking a leave of absence.

RJ

Rushabh R Joshi
CVS

🏠 📞 📹
home · call · FaceTime

December 1, 2016
10:14 AM **Incoming Call**   3 minutes

home
(615) 406-5972

FaceTime   📹 📞

After speaking with Rush, and following his directions of calling workers comp myself, I knew I needed to speak with someone else. It was clear that Rush did not know his job or the law and was giving me bad and erroneous directions. 36 minutes later, I texted Jefferson:

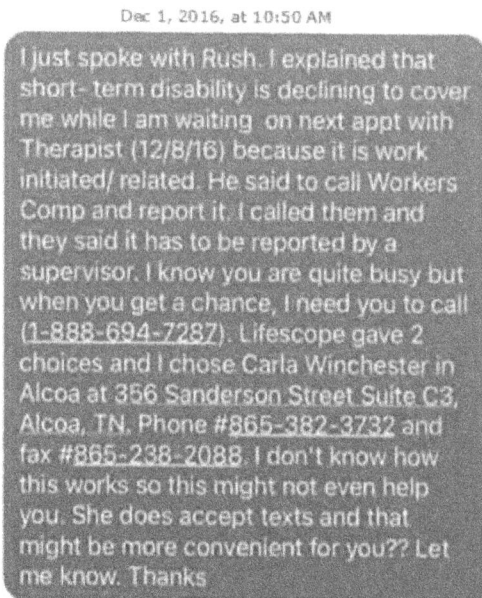

Dec 1, 2016, at 10:50 AM

> I just spoke with Rush. I explained that short- term disability is declining to cover me while I am waiting on next appt with Therapist (12/8/16) because it is work initiated/ related. He said to call Workers Comp and report it. I called them and they said it has to be reported by a supervisor. I know you are quite busy but when you get a chance, I need you to call (1-888-694-7287). Lifescope gave 2 choices and I chose Carla Winchester in Alcoa at 356 Sanderson Street Suite C3, Alcoa, TN. Phone #865-382-3732 and fax #865-238-2088. I don't know how this works so this might not even help you. She does accept texts and that might be more convenient for you?? Let me know. Thanks

I was out of work, with no money and no return date, but I was thrust into doing the job of my supervisors who apparently did not know their jobs or the law- now I had two to deal with and still no support.

Rush had previously set up a "GroupMe" August 31, 2016, at 8:57 **AM (THAT I REFUSED TO JOIN TO AID HIM IN HIS ABILITY TO INFRINGE UPON MY PERSONAL TIME).**

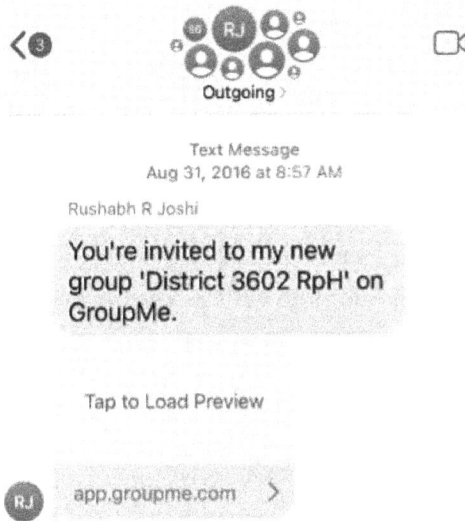

Text Message
Aug 31, 2016 at 8:57 AM

Rushabh R Joshi

You're invited to my new
group 'District 3602 RpH' on
GroupMe.

Tap to Load Preview

app.groupme.com

This was established to be able to reach multiple pharmacists at a time. I was notified of a text that was accidentally shared with all. I did not get the text because I refused the invitation from Rush when he initially set it up. He was already contacting me on my personal time off and I felt like this would be another unnecessary avenue for intrusion into my life by him. The text was important and reinforced everything I was saying about store 7246. It came from a floater:

Jani   Floater: Hey Rush, I'm going on vacation next week, but when I get back I was wondering if I could stay up in Newport for a couple of months. I (1/5)

think you have some older technicians who are making life hard for the new pharmacist and lead tech. Maybe with a little more stability up there the two (2/5) new people can have a chance to do the job you hired them for. When I've worked up in Newport in the past, I never had to babysit Debi Lindsay or Jolene (3/5)

but in the short time I've been there I too am growing frustrated and angry. Without going into a lot of detail now, I think I'm getting a pretty good (4/5)

frustrated and angry. Without going into a lot of detail now, I think I'm getting a pretty good (4/5)

read on the situation. I know they can work harder than they are now Thanks Jani (5/5)

Charlene Be careful who sees your msg..think everyone in district may see do to GroupMe..Charlene

I received no response from Jefferson, so I decided to fax all the information that I had found through research on the CVS HR site for employees. December 2, 2016, I faxed the following paperwork to Marge Ellen (secretary and district scheduler for Rush and Jefferson).

Marge Ellen,

(over plus 3

* Please forward to Jefferson/
Rush

Faxed 11 '16
12/2/16

Jefferson,

    I spoke to Rush about this. He gave me incorrect advice and told me to call it in. When I tried, I was told a supervisor has to (I can't call in my own) I tried to call you but it went straight to voicemail so I texted you the information to the best of my ability.

The Provider Lifescope gave as a choice is

    Carla Winchester
    366 Sanderson St
      Suite C3
      Alcoa, Tn

    Phone # 865 - 382 - 3932
    Fax # 865 - 238 - 2088

I don't know how this works but I guess you can use her. I received the LOA request in the mail and have faxed it to her today (12/2/16).

        DaDrda

* I found this information on myHR

TENNESSEE WORKERS' COMPENSATION INSURANCE POSTING NOTICE

The law requires this notice to be posted at the employer's place of business so all employees have access to it.

WHICH EMPLOYERS ARE COVERED BY THE TENNESSEE WORKERS' COMPENSATION ACT?

All employers with five (5) or more full or part-time employees, except as indicated below.
All employers engaged in the mining and production of coal with one (1) or more employees.
All workers in the construction industry unless they are specifically exempted.

WHAT SHOULD AN EMPLOYEE DO IF INJURED AT WORK?

1. Report the injury to the employer immediately;

2. Select a treating physician from a panel provided by the employer on the form described below. To report an injury contact:

   Store Manager or Immediate Supervisor
   Name of employer representative to notify in event of a work related injury

   1-888-694-7287
   Telephone number of employer representative to notify in event of a work related injury

   3416 Costa Hwy Newport Tn 37821
   Address of employer representative to notify in event of a work related injury

3. If you have questions or problems, contact the Bureau as indicated below.

WHAT SHOULD AN EMPLOYER DO WHEN AN INJURY IS REPORTED?

1. Immediately complete a First Report of Work Injury form and send it to the workers' compensation insurance company or the third party administrator; AND,

2. Offer the employee a panel of physicians. The physicians must be provided on the official state form, which is the "AGREEMENT BETWEEN EMPLOYER/EMPLOYEE CHOICE OF PHYSICIAN —Form C-42." Additional instructions are available on the form. The form is available at
   http://www.tn.gov/assets/entities/labor/attachments/c42.pdf

The Tennessee Bureau of Workers' Compensation has staff available to help both employees and employers For more information contact:

TENNESSEE BUREAU OF WORKERS' COMPENSATION
220 FRENCH LANDING DRIVE, 1-B
NASHVILLE, TENNESSEE 37243-1002
615-532-4812 OR TOLL FREE 800-332-2667
800-332-2257 (TDD)

http://www.tn.gov/workforce/section/injuries-at-work

LB-0922 (REV 7/15)   Authorization No. 337345   RDA 10183

The Tipping Point

Tennessee Bureau of Workers' Compensation
220 French Landing Drive, I-B
Nashville, TN 37243-1002

FORM C-42

EMPLOYER'S CHOICE OF PHYSICIAN

An employer must provide a partially-completed form listing at least three physicians to an employee upon the report of a workplace injury. The employee must complete and then sign and date the section below that indicates the physician chosen. A copy of the fully-completed form should be provided to the employee with the original kept on file by the employer. If the employee refuses to accept medical services from the chosen physician, the employee's rights to benefits may be delayed. **NOTE:** Employees traveling more than 15 miles one way to or from medical treatment may seek reimbursement of their travel expenses from the insurance carrier.

TO BE COMPLETED BY THE EMPLOYER:

Employer _____ Date of Injury 11/22/2016

Employer Contact _____ Phone _____ Email _____

Physician Name _____ Phone _____
Address _____ City _____ State ____ Zip _____

Physician Name _____ Phone _____
Address _____ City _____ State ____ Zip _____

Physician Name _____ Phone _____
Address _____ City _____ State ____ Zip _____

TO BE COMPLETED BY THE EMPLOYEE:

I have selected the following physician from the list provided to me by my employer:

Physician Name _____ Date Selected _____
Employee Name _____ Appt Date/Time _____
Address _____ City _____ State ____ Zip _____
Phone _____ Email _____
Employee Signature _____ Date _____

LB-0382 (REV 11/15)　　　　　　　　　　　RDA 10183

131

As I received feedback from the multiple agencies, I was directed to contact by Rush, I gained a lot of knowledge of the system. Most of the knowledge I gained would often be a little too late or met with resistance. I kept the paperwork to substantiate what I was telling Jefferson. November 28, 2016, Unum, the benefit administrator for short term disability that I had to personally file for, sent a letter.

The first part of the letter began as follows:

Unum
The Benefits Center PO Box 100158
Columbia, SC 29202-3158
Fax: 1-800-447-2498
www.unum.com

DAONDA PAYNE
REDACTED ST,
REDACTED TN

Dear Ms. Payne:

On **November 23, 2016,** we received a telephone call to initiate a Short-Term Disability claim and need additional information to continue our evaluation.

What We Need From You

Due to lack of contact information, we are unable to send the Attending Physician Statement to your physician. Please follow up with your physician to ensure that the attached form is completed and sent to us as soon as possible. It is important for us to receive this information to avoid a delay in the review of your claim. If the information is not received by December 19, 2016, we will be unable to continue our review of your claim.

The telephone call was from me as instructed by Rush to initiate my own claim.

December 12, 2016, UNUM wrote:

Unum
The Benefits Center PO Box 100158
Columbia, SC 29202-3158
Fax: 1-800-447-2498
www.unum.com

DAONDA PAYNE
REDACTED ST.
REDACTED. TN.

Dear Ms. Payne:

We have reviewed your **Short-Term Disability** claim and are **unable to approve** your request for benefits.

As you may know, your employer's plan states:

"WHAT DISABILITIES ARE NOT COVERED UNDER YOUR PLAN?"

"Benefits will not be paid for any **disabilities caused by, contributed to by,** or **resulting from,** your occupational sickness or injury unless you have made timely claim under the applicable worker's compensation law and have been denied a benefit, award, settlement or redemption under workers' law for such occupational sickness or injury and you meet all other eligibility requirements and definitions of disability under the Plan.

The contract further states: "**Occupational sickness** or injury means a sickness or injury that was caused by or **aggravated by any employment** for pay or profit."

In order to be eligible for Short Term Disability benefits under the plan as provided by your employer, the condition for which you are seeking benefits for, adjustment disorder with depression cannot be caused by, contributed to by, or resulting from your occupation as a pharmacy manager. The Attending Physician Statement completed by Carla Winchester, LCSW indicates your condition is work related. She indicates that conflicts with your supervisor and dissatisfaction with your job are barriers for your return to work. You reported issues at work causing an increase in symptoms resulting in your inability to work. Based on the above information, it has been determined that your condition is a work-related condition and cannot be supported under your employer's Short Term Disability plan.

I consulted with the counselor I was seeing through Lifescope, and she sent the necessary information to Unum. The Attending Physician Statement Behavioral Health for Unum included the diagnosis: **F43.21, Adjustment Disorder with Depression,** the fact that the condition was work related, a recommendation to stay at home effective November 29, 2016, with rationale for recommending disability leave, including conflicts with supervisor.

I did not get a copy of the diagnosis, nor did I know what the diagnosis was, or the comments made until I requested them to verify if John Moretta of Littler Mendelson (legal representative for CVS) or my attorney, Jarrel Wigger had requested and received the information. It was in December 2018, **two years later,** that I knew what was reported to Unum in 2016 and what was **sent to John Moretta in September of 2018.** It turned out that **my attorney never made a request which was also revealed in September 2018.**

I was getting nowhere with the paperwork I was filing and was getting no response from Rush or Jefferson. It was approaching Christmas, and I had no money. My bills continued to flow in, so I did what was necessary to pay them. I began to close smaller IRA's that I or my husband had prior to being employed with CVS.

On **December 12, 2016**, a **determination letter** was sent to me from **Unum** for the **short-term disability** that I had to file myself. The letter revealed that the claim I filed was ineligible to be paid as determined by the Attending Physician Statement from Carla Winchester, LCSW, through Lifescope. **The letter said:**

> "**Benefits will not be paid** for any disabilities caused by, contributed to by, or resulting from, your occupational sickness or injury **unless you have made a timely claim** under the applicable **workers' compensation law** and have been **denied a benefit, award, settlement, or redemption under workers' compensation** law for such occupational sickness or injury . . ."

> ". . . the condition for which you are seeking benefits for, adjustment disorder with depression cannot be caused by, contributed to by, or resulting from your occupation as a pharmacy manager. The Attending Physician Statement completed by Carla Winchester, LCSW indicates your **condition is work related.** She **indicates that conflicts with your supervisor and dissatisfaction with your job are barriers for your return to work.**"

The paperwork fiasco continued with me trying to get some sort of help. Still no response was given from my immediate supervisors. December 29, 2016, I received a call on my home phone from the Leave of Absence department that Rush instructed me to call and file my own claim.

Josh was calling to let me know that the process was not followed and what should have happened. What was "supposed to happen in that regard is that your supervisor is actually supposed to initiate a claim with workers comp or Gallagher Bassett." Surprise!!!!!! Rush violated the workers comp process entirely, but it appeared NOTHING WAS

DONE!!!!" This is just one example of how CVS cared about their employee and these actions should be considered when awarding any contracts to care for the public.

Readable Voicemail (**misspellings included by the BOT are left in the text for authenticity**):

(401) 765-1500

December 29, 2016

Hi this message is for Diana Payne my name is **Josh with leave of absence** Department with CBS. I'm actually just calling in regards to your continuous leave of absence **case number 204462** and the reason I'm calling is actually in regards to a letter received indication that due to you know not accepting the claim **due to be a workers comp claim. If you haven't been receiving any sort of payment.** So, what **supposed to happen** in that regard is that **your supervisor** is **actually supposed to initiate a claim with workers comp** or Gallagher Bassett. So, they can. So, you can at least get a letter indicating that if it is a workers comp claim that we which need to set up or work Scott leave. But if if you got a letter stating that the workers comp claim is denied then you they they would send you that letter to give to you know so you know **we can actually go ahead and process the payment.**

Unfortunately our department can actually reach out to gal.

37 Days had passed and at the time, I was unaware of the process of filing any sort of claim. I never intended to be in such a position; however, Rush initiated and forced the entire scenario. Unfortunately, his actions had consequences for me. I asked to be a floater, more than once beginning Friday, May 13 and now I was asking again but I was not granted my request. It appeared Rush would rather destroy a person

and their family life than come up with a solution. I would have taken a reassignment to a different district, but I just knew that was next to impossible since I could not even get a response from Rush or Jefferson.

The letter and the phone call educated me on whose responsibility it was to file.

The call (even though it was translated by a BOT) sounded almost painful for anyone to have to admit that "due to be a workers comp claim" . . . " So, what is supposed to happen in that regard is that your **supervisor** is actually **supposed to initiate** a claim with **workers comp** or Gallagher Bassett." The phone call was left on voicemail and was translated with the readable voicemail service provided by my cable company, so the messaging is a little broken, but Rush was in violation of Tennessee workers compensation laws. It was also clear that he did not even know the laws and was having me file my own claim. This is the United States of America and **He** was **responsible** for my **UNPAID LOA that he forced** instead of granting me a floater position or change of district. It was NEVER my idea to file for LOA as Mr. Moretta would try to push that narrative. This lie would be carried through 2022.

I was out of work and **forced** to take **LOA**. I had no money and was unable to work. I was still responsible for paying my company healthcare premiums and was notified by a billing notice on December 19, 2016, that I owed $1,665.97. I was not concerned about the bill because **I knew I could cover the costs with my FSA** account. **I was wrong. I was told that I could not use my FSA to pay Insurance premiums while I was on a LOA, but I was FORCED TO TAKE THE LOA BY RUSH!**

No one would listen. I continued to close the few individual IRA's that I hadn't already closed to pay for my insurance premiums and mortgage. I had to pay by January 1, 2017 or my insurance would be canceled! None of this was my fault but it did not matter: I was up against a corporation covering for the ineptitude of my supervisors. All I wanted to do was work! I spent the day after Christmas trying to contact anyone who could help. The LOA department was closed in observance of the holiday. I was instructed to pay out of pocket and file for **possible** reimbursement.

I continued to try to resolve matters, but I was getting nowhere. I reached out to my HR representative with no response.

From: dpayne@internet.com
Sent: Friday, December 30, 2016, 11:33 AM To: randall.hatfield2@ CVSCaremark.com Subject: LOA/Workers Comp

Randy,

Hello, my name is DaOnda Payne. I am a pharmacist with CVS at store #7246. I have been on a LOA since November and have not been cleared to return to work as Rushabh Joshi required. I have reached out to my short-term disability (UNUM) and have completed all steps required by them to at least receive some sort of income. It was determined by UNUM that they could not pay due to the fact it was solely a work-related incident.

I reached out to Rushabh Joshi, Pharmacy Supervisor on December 1, 2016, at 8:36am to let him know that short-term disability declined and said it had to be processed through Workers Comp. He told me to call it in (which we all know is not the procedure) so I did. During the conversation with Workers Comp at 1-888-694-7287. They told me I could not call my own in, but I was following the instructions of my Immediate Supervisor, Rushabh Joshi. I then went to MyHr on our employee website and printed the Tennessee Workers Compensation Insurance Posting Notice along with the Form C-42 and faxed it to Marge Ellen on December 2, 2016, at 11:46am to forward to Jefferson Gates and Rushabh Joshi, hoping this would help them be COMPLIANT with the procedure that needed to be followed. Included in that fax was a note that read as such:

Jefferson,

I spoke to Rush about this. He gave me incorrect advice and told me to call it in. When I tried, I was told a supervisor has to (I can't call in my own). I tried to call you, but it went straight to voicemail, so I texted you the information to the best of my ability. The provider Lifescope gave as a choice is:

Carla Winchester
356 Sanderson Street Suite C3 Alcoa, TN
Ph # 865-382-3732
Fax # 865-238-2088

I don't know how this works, but I guess you can use her. I received the LOA request in the mail and have faxed it to her today, 12/2/2016.

DaOnda

*I found this information on my HR
I texted Marge Ellen on December 2. 2016 at 10:24am to make sure my faxes reached the office and were forwarded to Jefferson/Rush, and she confirmed they had been, and **she placed them on Rushabh Joshi's desk** and that Jefferson did not have cell phone service in the office was why he didn't answer.

I have been trying to follow procedures as outlined by CVS, but I have heard nothing and have had no income since the first ending pay period in December. I faxed a letter along with everything that I forwarded to Rush and Jefferson to myHR at 1-847-554-1731 on 12/20/2016 at 12:52PM. I just heard back from them on 12/29/2016 at 1:54PM to say they could not help me to reach out to my immediate supervisor (which I have done) and they gave me your e-mail as an alternate. I have had no income and can no longer keep drawing from my 401k that I had previous to CVS. If I don't hear anything today, I am calling the Tennessee Bureau of Workers' Compensation number on the Posting. I don't know what else to do and need to survive. Thank you for any assistance you can provide.

DaOnda Payne
Pharmacy Manager Store #7246

I had applied for a position as a contracting pharmacist online. I did not know what that entailed but it was a 3-month assignment. I needed a source of income to live, and I had a brother who would provide me with a place to stay. I had been looking for a way out, but I did not know I was going to have to leave my home and family to continue contributing financially.

I received the call for the job in December. The date was not important to me but would be in two years. I continued to try to work with my supervisors (although I never got any useful responses if any response at all). I began going through the onboarding process for the 3-month job. I thought I could do that with the support of my family. My brother provided me with a place that was fully furnished so all I had to do was take a few clothes for each week- simple. It was anything but simple emotionally.

The position was for a staff pharmacist at Wright Patterson Air Force Base for the Department of Defense. In my mind, that was a dream job with respect and discipline. I needed to work, **this was a temporary position**, and I could still try to get my supervisors to let me come back to work. That would never happen, and it would be laid out by Mr. Moretta as though I completely planned the whole thing. I am quite certain that no one plans to take a pay cut OF $25.02/HOUR, drive 2 states away to work and leave their families as a well thought out plan (ludicrous).

I completed each step of the onboarding process as I was seeing Carla and talked to her about my situation. She offered to put me on indefinite leave but that was not going to help my financial situation nor my work predicament with Rush. I was hoping that someone would come to their senses before I had to take the job and move-that never happened.

I wrote to Randall Hatfield in HR several times in an attempt to get help. Finally, January 2, 2017, One Month, one week and 4 days (41 days) after the recorded date of the "injury," "Randy" wrote back:

On Jan 2, 2017. At 2:47 PM, Hatfield, Randall R. Randall.Hatfield@ CVSHealth.com wrote:

Thanks for providing me with your information. I will have Jefferson and Rush submit as a Worker's Compensation claim. This will go to a 3rd. party vendor for further review.

Thanks, Randy H.

My efforts were hopeless!!!! I was suffering from adjustment disorder with depression (F43.21) and this was not helping. I had no idea what was going on.

January 5, 2017, one month and two weeks (44 days) later, I received this from AIG:
***" The purpose of this notice is to request that you contact us immediately if you start losing time from work for any reason associated with this accident as well as for the following reasons noted below:

*Your physician takes you off work completely as a result of this accident and/or" . . .

To add insult to injury, I received a letter from Sedgwick Claims Management Services, Inc. on January 6, 2017, one day later. Apparently, the paperwork filed by Rush and/or Jefferson, must have been filed inaccurately.

I reviewed the letter and fell further into the massive depression hole. Again, it stated "if you lose time at work due to your work-related injury, please let me know **right away.**" I was doomed. I was EMOTIONALLY dying, and these people were digging my grave. I did the only thing that I could do to survive; I left home and went to Wright Patterson Air Force Base and reported for duty with no other choice. I wrote to Ms. Sanders OF SEDGWICK claims for workers compensation. In the letter, I explained to her "I noticed in the letter my Social Security Number (at least the last 4) is incorrect so I will not be signing anything until correct." I never heard another word. No one was punished and nothing changed, **I would find out two years later.**

I worked for a week before I could accept the fact that I had to leave my career and my family behind. I finally brought myself to send a resignation letter to Rush. I was given the strength and reassurance through Martin Luther King Jr. I was home for the holiday from work as I wrote my resignation letter.

Resignation
January 15, 2017, at 6:29 PM

Rushabh,
It is with great sadness that I end my lengthy and successful career with CVS today. The treatment I have received has caused much turmoil in my life. I know you said to me that you would be surprised at what you can say/do when you take emotion out of it, but we were given emotions for a reason. Maybe the "smoke screens" you spoke of are clearing and you can now see the truth.

> **"Our lives begin to end the day we become silent about things that matter."**
> Martin Luther King, Jr.

DaOnda Payne

It was not over for me by a long shot. I e-mailed Randy Hatfield in HR:

January 29, 2017

Randall Hatfield

Human Resources Business Partner/Recruiter/SR. Advisor at CVS Health- Tennessee, Kentucky, and Southwest Virginia

Randy,
On January 15, 2017, I e-mailed my letter of resignation to Rushabh Joshi. As stated in that letter, it was with great sadness that I had to end my long successful career with CVS due to the treatment I have received and the turmoil it has caused in my life. I want it to be known that the level of satisfaction that Rushabh Joshi experiences with his manipulation of situations and condescending behavior is appalling. He once bragged to me that you would be amazed at what you can say/do when you take emotion out of it.

That behavior is not consistent with the values I have come to know as an employee at CVS. As you stated on your profile page, CVS Health is an innovative, fast-growing company guided by values that focus on teamwork, integrity, and respect for our colleagues and customers. I would like to point out that I too am/was a colleague who received very little respect from this man. I have taken steps to protect my license/ability to continue in my career in a truly professional and respectful atmosphere that will not jeopardize my integrity.

I have been given very little support/guidance from my immediate supervisor, so I am relying on you to step in. I tried to call to get the process started to have my 401k rolled over to my Edward Jones account with no success. They informed me **Friday, January 27, 2017,** that I am **still active,** and I would have to call back! I have received no help on behalf of CVS to survive and I would greatly appreciate it if I could access my money to do so. If you can get this matter straightened out and get the proper paperwork started, I may be able to take care of my financial obligations and relieve some of the turmoil this has created. I cannot be reached M- F 9–6 except during lunch break, so any correspondence needs to be scheduled to not interfere with my current employment.

Thank you, DaOnda Payne

> On Jan 30, 2017, at 10:00 AM, Hatfield, Randall R. <Randall.Hatfield@CVSHealth.com> wrote:
>
> Our 401k is managed by Future Funds. To rollover, you can also visit the Future Fund site to obtain a rollover form.
>
> Future Fund Contact Center
> 888-694-7287 (888-MY-HR-CVS)
>
> Mailing Address
> CVS Future Fund Contact Center
> P.O. Box 199713-9712
> Dallas, TX 75219
>
> Thanks.
> Randy H.

Randy obviously did not read or pay attention to the content of my email and simply sent me the information on who manages 401k accounts. **Two hours and 27 minutes later**, I sent a simple condensed email to Randy:

From: DaOnda Payne; dpayne@internet.com
Subject: Re: Employment status-401k rollover
Date: Jan. 30, 2017, 12:28:08PM
To: Hatfield, Randall Randall.Hatfield@CVSHealth.com

They have to be notified of status change before they will talk to me. I tried Friday.

I tried another way 23 minutes later:

From: DaOnda Payne; dpayne@internet.com
Subject: Re: Employment status-401k rollover
Date: Jan. 30, 2017, 12:50:04PM
To: Hatfield, Randall Randall.Hatfield@CVSHealth.com Randy,

I just tried AGAIN and was told it can take 7–10 days for my status to update but as of NOW, I am still active. Since it has been that long since I have resigned, that would lead me to believe that either you (Human Resources) or Rushabh Joshi has failed to efficiently initiate my status change. Any help you may give would be greatly appreciated. Thank you,

DaOnda Payne
Sent from my iPhone.

* January 30 minus (7–10 days) = January 20, 2017.
     If Rush had properly completed paperwork, I would NOT still be ACTIVE. I resigned on January 15, 2017.

One hour and 37 minutes later:

On Jan 30, 2017, at 2:27 PM, Hatfield, Randall R.
<Randall.Hatfield@CVSHealth.com>wrote:
I've escalated.
Thanks, Randy H.
I waited until **February 1, 2017 (two days later)** and tried again:

From: DaOnda Payne; dpayne@internet.com
Subject: Re: Employment status-401k rollover
Date: Feb 1,2017, 12:43:23 PM

Randy,

I called Future Fund just a few minutes ago and my status has FINALLY updated. However, I cannot request a final distribution of MY funds until February 16, 2017, and it will not process until 3/25/2017. I have read the rules and am aware of the process, so I asked what my **SEPARATION DATE** was. To my surprise, it is recorded as **January 31, 2017,** which is **incorrect. I resigned and e-mailed my resignation to Rushabh Joshi 2 weeks prior to that.** I would appreciate a correction so I can request a final distribution sooner.

Thank you for your time and attention to this matter.

DaOnda Payne
Sent from my iPhone.

one of two things occurred:

Either Rush did not read and acknowledge my resignation, or he did and once again, he did not know or do his job.

This story is my destiny. I want to shine a light on more than the poor working conditions pharmacists face. I want to show the hidden, often mental abuse, that is incurred when no longer considered valuable by this company. I hope to make the difference that so many have failed to accomplish. The timing is right with the new CEO Karen Lynch in place. Maybe she will make that change that is so desperately needed. I was fortunate and survived where many have not. I was attacked from all sides and began to know the meaning of "what does not kill you, makes you stronger."

Seeking Justice

I was read to during the Code Red meeting, but **THESE state-ments were NEVER read to me.** The following are **REAL STATEMENTS written by employees** (grammatical errors included). CVS was aware of the contents and the hostility exposed by the state-ments but that did not stop them from sending me back to the store with a clear message of *ZERO TOLERANCE.* **I did not see these until 2 years later.**

F43.21 Adjustment Disorder with Depression

Symptoms

Although depression may occur only once during your life, people typically have multiple episodes. During these episodes, symptoms occur most of the day, nearly every day and may include:

- Feelings of sadness, tearfulness, emptiness or hopelessness

- Angry outbursts, irritability or frustration, even over small matters

- Loss of interest or pleasure in most or all normal activities, such as sex, hobbies or sports

- Sleep disturbances, including insomnia or sleeping too much

- Tiredness and lack of energy, so even small tasks take extra effort

- Reduced appetite and weight loss or increased cravings for food and weight gain

- Anxiety, agitation or restlessness

- Slowed thinking, speaking or body movements

- Feelings of worthlessness or guilt, fixating on past failures or self-blame

- Trouble thinking, concentrating, making decisions and remembering things

- Frequent or recurrent thoughts of death, suicidal thoughts, suicide attempts or suicide

- Unexplained physical problems, such as back pain or headaches

For many people with depression, symptoms usually are severe enough to cause noticeable problems in day-to-day activities, such as work, school, social activities or relationships with others. Some people may feel generally miserable or unhappy without really knowing why.

Page 7

```
1     (9:16 A.M.)
2               DaONDA PAYNE,
3     called as a witness and having been first duly
4     sworn, was examined and testified as follows:
5               EXAMINATION
6     BY MR. MORETTA:
7          Q   Good morning, Ms. Payne. I
8     introduced myself earlier, but I will do so again
9     for the record. My name is John Moretta, and I
10    represent CVS Rx Services, Inc.,
```

To be continued in Book 2, *Seeking Justice.*

148

About the Author

*M*y name is DaOnda Marie Payne, and I am always kidding about my name. My typical story is, "I am number 11 out of 12 children and my parents ran out of names!" Truth is, I am number 11 of 12 children with a heavy influence from my late father, Clarence Combs. He did not have a middle name but that did not matter. He made a name for himself as an Army veteran who served in World War II and a sixth-grade graduate from Knott County, Kentucky that went on to become a UAW, union, Vice President.

As a union Vice President of Local 87 in Ohio for auto workers, he devoted his efforts to protect their rights and ensure they had healthcare and benefits. As a Pharmacist, I wish I had someone like him to fight for me. I never dreamed I would fall victim to what the Civil Rights act of 1964 was trying to protect but I did. I hope my suffering at the hands of CVS healthcare corporation will shine a light on what can and does happen and make a difference for pharmacists like he did for the auto workers. This treatment has to end.

Endnotes

1 The mental health crisis of working moms (cvshealth.com) https://www.cvshealth.com/news/news-and-insights.html?topic=Mental%20Health, October 26, 2022, | Mental Health

2 CVS Health CEO interview: Karen Lynch on 'taking up space' | Fortune, https://fortune.com/2023/03/08/cvs-health-ceo-karen-lynch-oak-street-signify-primary-care-t-shirt-taking-up-space/. BYFORTUNE EDITORS, March 8, 2023, at 5:10 PM EST

3 CVS 'gender transition' guide says employees must use preferred pronouns, can use bathroom reflecting identity. https://www.foxbusiness.com/economy/cvs-gender-transition-guide-employees-preferred-pronouns-bathroom-reflecting-identity#:~:text=CVS,Landon%20Mion%20FOXBusiness By Landon Mion FOXBusiness Published April 15, 2023, 10:00am EDT.

4 Leading Health Solutions Company | CVS health, https://www.cvshealth.com/news/mental-health/its-ok-to-get-help.html

5 Pharmacist Burnout and Stress (uspharmacist.com) https://www.uspharmacist.com/article/pharmacist-burnout-and-stress

6 Rebecca Knight—Insider (businessinsider.com)

7 John B. Moretta | Littler Mendelson P.C., https://www.littler.com/people/john-b-moretta

8   Attorney Jarrel Wigger | Managing Attorney at Wigger Law Firm | North Charleston SC | Attorney Near Mehttps://www.wiggerlawfirm .com/attorney-jarrel-wigger.php

9   Are CVS' metrics unfairly eliminating older pharmacists? (drugtopics.com), https://www.drugtopics.com/view/are-cvs-metrics -unfairly-eliminating-older-pharmacists

10 61140—Board of Pharmacy (tnsosfiles.com), https://publications .tnsosfiles.com/rules/1140/1140-03.20170220.pdf

11 Tennessee Department of Health: Licensure Verification (tn.gov), https://apps.health.tn.gov/Licensure/default.aspx, 1140—Board of Pharmacy (tnsosfiles.com), https://publications.tnsosfiles.com /rules/1140/1140.htm

12 Tennessee Department of Health: Licensure Verification (tn.gov), https://apps.health.tn.gov/Licensure/default.aspx

www.ingramcontent.com/pod-product-compliance
Lightning Source LLC
Chambersburg PA
CBHW031548260326
41914CB00002B/320